The First Book of
WordPerfect® 5.1

RELATED TITLES

The Best Book of WordStar® (Features Release 5.0)
Vincent Alfieri

The Best Book of WordPerfect® 5.1
Vincent Alfieri, Revised by Ralph Blodgett

The Best Book of Microsoft® Word 5
Kate Miller Barnes

The Best Book of dBase IV™
Joseph-David Carrabis

Understanding Microsoft® Windows
Katherine Stuart Ewing

The First Book of Microsoft® Word 5
Brent D. Helsop and David Angell

The First Book of Paradox® 3
Jonathan Kamin

The First Book of PC Tools® Deluxe
Gordon McComb

The First Book of Quicken
Gordon McComb

Understanding MS-DOS, Second Edition
Kate O'Day, John Angermeyer, Revised by Harry Henderson

Understanding NetWare®
Stan Schatt

The Best Book of: Lotus® 1-2-3®, Third Edition, Release 2.2
Alan Simpson

The Best Book of: DOS
Alan Simpson

The First Book of Lotus® 1-2-3® Release 2.2
Alan Simpson and Paul Lichtman

The First Book of The Norton Utilities
Joseph Wikert
(forthcoming)

The First Book of Microsoft® Works for the PC
Ruth Witkin

For the retailer nearest you, or to order directly from the publisher, call 800-257-5755. International orders telephone 609-461-6500.

The First Book of

WordPerfect® 5.1

Kate Barnes

A Division of Macmillan Computer Publishing

11711 North College, Carmel, Indiana 46032 USA

To Jeff
Thanks, friend.

FIRST EDITION
FIFTH PRINTING—1991

International Standard Book Number: 0-672-27307-1
Library of Congress Catalog Card Number: 90-64233

Acquisitions Editor: *Richard K. Swadley*
Development Editor: *Marie Butler-Knight*
Manuscript Editor: *Don MacLaren*
Production Coordinator: *Becky Imel*
Illustrators: *T.R. Emrick, Don Clemons*
Cover Art: *Held & Diedrich Design*
Production: *Dan Armstrong, Brad Chinn, Sally Copenhaver, Bill Hurley, Lori Lyons, Jennifer Matthews, Dennis Sheehan, Mary Beth Wakefield*
Indexer: *Sharon Hilgenberg*
Technical Reviewer: *Shannon Cotton, WordPerfect Corporation*

Printed in the United States of America

Contents

3   *Getting Around with Menus, Keyboard, and Mouse, 23*

vi

4   *Working with Words, 37*

5   *Deleting, Copying, and Moving Text, 47*

viii

xi

Preface

Popular word processors usually have over 150 features for you to learn to use. This is more than the average user needs or wants, and, for the beginning user, the sheer bulk can be intimidating.

What *The First Book of WordPerfect 5.1* does is glean only the "most used" features. It focuses on those features you'll need to use in the great majority of your work. This way, you save time and eliminate the frustration of trying to sort out what you need from what you don't need.

The approach is meant to be simple. Such aids as quick steps to operations, overviews, everyday examples, and plentiful screen illustrations are designed for the beginning user. It's a simple, short book to make your learning of WordPerfect short and simple.

xiii

Trademark Acknowledgments

All terms mentioned in this book that are known to be trademarks or service marks are listed below. In addition, terms suspected are capitalized. SAMS cannot attest to the accuracy of this information. Use of a term in this book should not be regarded as affecting the validity of any trademark or service mark.

Lotus 1-2-3 is a registered trademark of Lotus Development Corporation.

MultiMate is a registered trademark of Microsoft Corporation.

WordPerfect is a registered trademark of WordPerfect Corporation.

Chapter 1

Getting Ready to Use WordPerfect

In This Chapter

▶ *What word processing is*
▶ *Which computer system components you'll use*
▶ *How to create a document*

Word Processing Made Easy

Though you may want to fire up your computer and begin punching keys *right now*, if you spend just a few moments picking up some basic understandings, you'll avoid confusion later on. Once you have the "big picture," you can fill in the details.

Word processing is the term used to describe the development of letters, reports, and other documents with a computer. Word processing offers many advantages versus handwriting or typing documents. Speed is a primary advantage. Because most people handwrite at about twelve words per minute, you don't have to be a speed demon on a keyboard to improve your efficiency with word processing. Another advantage you gain with word processing is the ease of entry, editing, and printing your work. You replace the cumbersome "cut, paste, and retype" approach with copying, moving, and deleting words instantly. A final, printed copy is only a few keystrokes away. The printed copy is clean and free of erasures and whiteout.

WordPerfect is one brand of word processor. It has been a best seller for years because of its simplicity and power. You'll no doubt begin using it to create small and straightforward documents. But once you get up and running and want to go on to more sophisticated word processing, WordPerfect won't hold you back.

The written works you create using WordPerfect are called *documents*. A document can be any written element you create—a letter, a report, a memo, an expense sheet, a bill, or a list (to name just a few). You can combine elements in one document (such as following a letter with a bill). You decide how many documents you want to create and the contents of each document.

2

Computer System Components

WordPerfect can only be used with an appropriate computer system. This book describes using WordPerfect with an IBM-compatible microcomputer (also known as a personal computer). *IBM compatible* is the standard set by IBM which other (often less expensive) computers match in specifications. Not all IBM-compatible computers are completely compatible, so if you notice a difference in processing from that described in this book, it may be that your computer is not perfectly compatible. If you're concerned about this, ask your computer dealer.

Your computer system includes *hardware* and *software*. Hardware is made up of the computer parts you can see and touch. Figure 1-1 illustrates these hardware components:

► *Keyboard*: The component that resembles the keys on a typewriter with a few added. You'll "talk" to your computer (and to WordPerfect) through your keyboard. By pressing certain keys you send messages to the computer. You also use the keyboard to type in documents.

▶ *Monitor*: The component that looks like a television screen. You can see the results of keyboard entries on the monitor. The text you type in also appears. WordPerfect will send you messages on the monitor if it doesn't understand what you have entered or if you need more information to continue. Carefully read the messages when they appear. This is WordPerfect's only means of communicating with you.

▶ *Central Processing Unit* (*CPU*): The CPU is typically the most difficult hardware component for a beginner to understand. The wonders of word processing take place within the CPU. Inside is active memory (called *random-access memory* [*RAM*]). The documents you are using and necessary parts of WordPerfect are stored in RAM as you work. The documents remain in RAM as long as the computer is turned on. When the computer is turned off (or the power is accidentally cut), the documents are lost from RAM. This is why it is so important to save your work regularly as you go. Otherwise, an unexpected power failure could cause you to lose valuable work.

▶ *Hard Disks, Floppy Disks, and Disk Drives*: When you save your work, it is transferred from RAM to a disk for permanent storage. Once your work is saved on a disk, you can turn off your computer and retrieve the document from the disk when you use WordPerfect again. The disk may be a hard disk, which is fixed in the CPU. Or the disk may be a 5 1/4" or 3 1/2" floppy (flexible) disk. Floppies are removable from a disk drive in the computer. This disk drive is used to copy documents to and from RAM.

▶ *Printer* (optional): You can use WordPerfect without a printer, but if you do, you can only view your documents on the monitor. You cannot get a hard copy of your work without a printer.

▶ *Mouse* (optional): You can use a mouse to point to and select WordPerfect options as a substitute for making selections from the keyboard. However, you will still use the keyboard for entering text and for some WordPerfect functions. Many WordPerfect users prefer a mouse because it seems to be easier and faster to use than the keyboard. This choice is a matter of individual taste and skill.

3

▶ *Cables*: Hardware components must be linked using the cable supplied by your computer dealer.

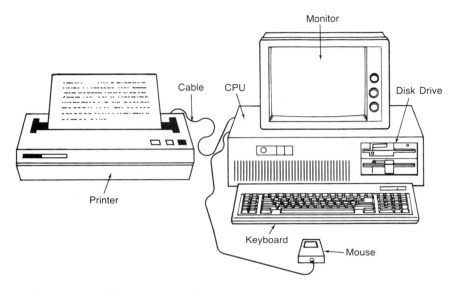

4

Figure 1-1. Hardware components

Before using your computer, make sure the cables are in place, the hardware is turned on, and, if you are using a printer, the printer has paper installed.

As you use your computer, observe these basic maintenance rules:

▶ Store disks at common office temperatures.

▶ Keep your environment clean and free from dust.

▶ Periodically clean the disk drives.

▶ Use the supplied labels with disks and write on disks with felt-tip pens (not ball-point pens or sharp pencils).

▶ Don't touch the exposed magnetic portion of the disk (housed inside the plastic cover).

▶ Don't spill liquids on the computer.

▶ Don't expose the disks to magnets.

▶ Always treat the computer with TLC (tender loving care). It is built to last but, like any electronic device, can be jarred or broken if misused.

Computer software contains the instructions to the computer and the text or data that make the process function. WordPerfect is considered a software product. The instructions that make up WordPerfect are stored as *files* with identifying names. You'll store your documents on disk, too, and give them identifying names. (A document is the equivalent of a file.) The software that allows WordPerfect to operate with your computer hardware is called the *operating system*. In this case, you'll be using DOS, which stands for Disk Operating System.

How You Create a Document

Now that you have a broad view of the computer hardware and software, we'll take a look at the overall process you'll use to create a document with WordPerfect. The remaining chapters in this book cover the details of these major steps.

To start, you'll install WordPerfect on your computer. Installing the program means that the files on the WordPerfect disks are placed on your computer or on a disk for your daily use. Installation only needs to be done once. Once WordPerfect is installed on your computer, start up WordPerfect. Certain settings, called *defaults*, are already fixed in WordPerfect, but they can be changed. For example, the left and right margins are defaulted to 1″ each. You can change the margins to the size you desire.

Once you have started WordPerfect, use the *menus* to select what you want to do. Menus are lists of options you have. Figure 1-2 shows a menu. Once you become familiar with WordPerfect functions, you may want to skip the menus and enter your selections via keystrokes.

Type in the document. As you work, a small, blinking mark called the *cursor* marks your position on the screen. Figure 1-3 shows the cursor under the "t" in the word "typist." When you use a mouse, the *pointer* appears to mark your location. Figure 1-4 shows the mouse pointer indicating "t" in "typist."

In addition to the text you enter, you may choose certain format options. The word "format" refers to the appearance of

5

```
┌──────────────────────────────────────────────────────────────────┐
│ ▓File▓ Edit Search Layout Mark Tools Font Graphics Help            │
│ ┌──────────────┐                                                   │
│ │▓Retrieve▓    │─────────────────────────────────────────────     │
│ │ Save         │                                                   │
│ │ Text In    ▸ │                                                   │
│ │ Text Out   ▸ │                                                   │
│ │ Password   ▸ │                                                   │
│ ├──────────────┤                                                   │
│ │ List Files   │                                                   │
│ │ Summary      │                                                   │
│ ├──────────────┤                                                   │
│ │ Print        │                                                   │
│ ├──────────────┤                                                   │
│ │ Setup      ▸ │                                                   │
│ ├──────────────┤                                                   │
│ │ Goto DOS     │                                                   │
│ │ Exit         │                                                   │
│ └──────────────┘                                                   │
│                                                                    │
│                                        Doc 1 Pg 1 Ln 1" Pos 1"     │
└──────────────────────────────────────────────────────────────────┘
```

Figure 1-2. A sample menu

```
┌──────────────────────────────────────────────────────────────────┐
│ File Edit Search Layout Mark Tools Font Graphics Help              │
│ ─────────────────────────────────────────────────────────────     │
│ The typist is going                                                │
│                                                                    │
│                                                                    │
│                                                                    │
│                                                                    │
│                                                                    │
│                                                                    │
│                                                                    │
│                                                                    │
│                                                                    │
│                                        Doc 1 Pg 1 Ln 1" Pos 2.9"   │
└──────────────────────────────────────────────────────────────────┘
```

Figure 1-3. The keyboard cursor

```
File Edit Search Layout Mark Tools Font Graphics Help
The Typist is going

                                        Doc 1 Pg 1 Ln 1" Pos 2.9"
```

Figure 1-4. The mouse pointer

your text on the screen and when printed. WordPerfect has a wide variety of format options, including tabs to indent the first line of a paragraph, margins to determine how much white space will surround the printed text, page numbers, and character formats (such as underlines and bold text). Each of these formats is shown in Figure 1-5.

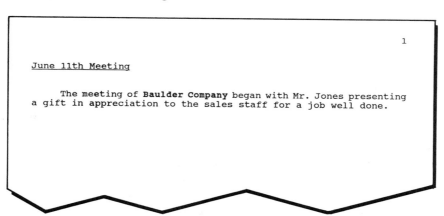

Figure 1-5. Tabs, margins, page numbers, underlined text, and bold text

Save your work. Saving a document copies it from temporary storage in your computer to permanent storage on a disk. Do this regularly as you go to protect your work from a power loss. Always save your work before you leave WordPerfect.

Next, spell check your document. Most WordPerfect users wait until they think the document is fully developed before spell checking it. That way, they don't have to spell check the document again because of extensive editing.

Generate any special aids such as an index or table of contents. This is the last act to perform on your document because the changes made during editing or spell checking may change the page numbers tied to the aid. Save your work again. (You can never save too often.)

Print the document. Actually, you can print a draft of your document at any time. Some users like to see a draft as they work just to ensure the formatting is to their liking.

Exit WordPerfect after you have saved your work and are done using WordPerfect. When you start up WordPerfect again, the document you've saved is available for retrieval and further editing.

Here again are the steps you take to create a document once WordPerfect is installed on your computer:

▶ Start up WordPerfect.
▶ Make selections via the menu.
▶ Type in your document (the cursor marks your spot on the monitor screen).
▶ Enter formatting (such as tabs and margins).
▶ Save the document—often.
▶ Spell check the document.
▶ Generate special aids (such as an index or table of contents).
▶ Save the work again.
▶ Print the document.
▶ Exit WordPerfect. (You can retrieve the saved document later through WordPerfect.)

Through this book you'll learn the many nuances of this overall process of creating a document. The basic process is still the same, however, regardless of how fancy or plain or how long or short your document is. Just invest a little time, follow the process, exercise a smidgen of patience, and you'll be successfully word processing with WordPerfect in no time.

Summary

In this chapter you've learned:

- ► Word processing is a generic term that refers to the creation of any type of word-laden document on a computer.
- ► The benefits of word processing are speed, ease of editing, and clean printing.
- ► Documents are the work you create with WordPerfect.
- ► Hardware comprises the computer components you can see and touch.
- ► Before starting, make sure the cables are connected, the hardware is turned on, and paper is available for the printer.
- ► Follow the procedures for taking care of hardware and magnetic media.
- ► Software includes operating system, WordPerfect, and document files. These files are stored on disk.

9

Chapter 2

Using WordPerfect with Your Computer

In This Chapter

▶ *How to put WordPerfect on your computer*
▶ *How to start up WordPerfect*

Installing WordPerfect

When you buy WordPerfect, it is delivered with a manual and several disks. Before you can use WordPerfect for the first time, you must ready WordPerfect for your computer. This is called *installing* WordPerfect. This is a one-time operation; once Word-Perfect is available, you can use it again and again.

Because the folks at WordPerfect have you—the first-time user—in mind, the installation process is pretty much auto-mated. You need only know a little about the type of computer you are using and how to use your keyboard to respond to the screens WordPerfect shows you.

Your Type of Computer

Regardless of the brand of computer you are using, it will fit into one of three categories. Make sure you know the category in which your computer fits.

- ▶ *Hard Disk* (single user): You have a hard disk in the computer with one or more disk drives. WordPerfect will be stored on the hard disk.
- ▶ *Floppy Disk* (single user): This type of system uses floppy-disk drives only. You do not have a hard disk inside the machine for storing files and documents. WordPerfect resides on a floppy disk as you work.
- ▶ *Network* (multiple users): Your system hooks several computers into a primary computer. The primary computer is called the *server* and has a hard disk to hold WordPerfect. That copy of WordPerfect is shared by all the computers attached to the server.

12

Formatting Disks

When you buy a floppy disk, it could be used by any number of types of computers and types of operating systems. *Formatting* a floppy disk makes that disk ready to be used by your operating system and your computer.

If you are using a floppy-disk system, you will use floppy disks to hold WordPerfect and your documents. Before installing WordPerfect, you will need at least ten formatted disks on hand. If you are using a hard disk or working on a network, you will want to format floppy disks to store additional "backup" copies of your documents. You don't need these to install WordPerfect, but it's always a good idea to have several extra formatted floppy disks on which you can save your work.

> ⊘ **Caution:** When you format a floppy disk, all the information on the disk is erased. *Never* format a floppy disk if you want to save the information on the disk.

To format a floppy disk using the DOS operating system, make sure DOS is available. On a two-drive system, put the DOS disk in drive A (which is typically the top or left drive). On a hard-disk system, DOS already should be installed on your computer. If it is not, see your computer dealer.

With DOS available, go to the *system prompt* for the drive where DOS resides. The system prompt is usually A for the A drive on a floppy-disk system or C for the C (hard-disk) drive. If another letter currently appears, just type in the letter of the desired drive and then a colon. Then press the Enter key (often marked Return or with a left-pointing arrow with a tail). For example, to go to the C drive, you would type this in

```
C:
```

and press Enter.

Once the system prompt appears, make sure you have a disk in the available floppy drive. (On a two-drive system this will be the B [right or lower] drive. On a hard-disk system, this will be the A [upper or only] drive.) Type in the format command to "command" DOS to format the disk in that drive. The command is *format*, followed by the drive letter where the floppy disk to be formatted resides, and then a colon. For example, you would use the following command from the hard disk C drive to format the floppy disk in drive A.

```
format A:
```

Press Enter. You are asked if you really want to format the disk in the drive. *Take time to check the drive letter.* Make sure the correct drive is identified.

Caution: If you format the wrong disk, the contents of that disk will be wiped out. For example, you can accidentally format your hard disk and wipe out all your software and documents. Be careful! Always double check that you are formatting the right disk in the right drive.

When you are sure you are formatting the correct disk, press *y* (for Yes) to continue the format process.

Now you just wait while the computer processes. You can tell it is working by the lights and the sound of the machine. A message like "format another?" appears when the process is complete. Press *y* (for Yes) to format another disk or *n* (for No) to stop formatting disks.

Q Formatting a Disk

1. From your DOS prompt, type in a command like *Format A:* and press Enter.

    A message appears asking if you want to format the disk in the drive indicated.

2. Make sure you correctly identified the drive with the disk to format. The contents (if any) of the disk will be erased. Press *y* if the command is correct.

    The computer processes and a message appears when it is finished.

14

Directories

If you are using a hard disk or are part of a network, you'll need to understand the concept of directories. If you are using a floppy drive system, you should at least skim this part. That way, when words like "directories" and "paths" are mentioned later, they won't confuse you.

A disk can be divided into parts called *directories*. Directories are especially useful on hard disks to keep certain types of files separate so that you can easily find what you need. For example, Figure 2-1 shows a diagram representing the directories on a hard disk. Directories take on the structure of an upside-down tree. The first level is called the *root*. The root is represented by a slash. Off the root, typically, is a directory for your operating system along with directories for your software. In Figure 2-1, the operating system is DOS and the software includes WordPerfect (WP51) and Lotus 1-2-3 (123). Notice that the names for the directories, while abbreviated, help identify the software.

When you install WordPerfect, it will automatically make a directory for you, if you wish. This avoids a lot of hassle for you and is particularly helpful for beginners. Also, when you begin using WordPerfect with a hard disk, you'll probably place your own documents on the same directory as the Word-Perfect files and identify them with special naming techniques, which we'll discuss in this book. Later, if you want to add a directory under WordPerfect and place your documents there, you can. To do so, consult your operating system manual for how to make directories and copy documents between directories.

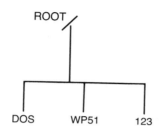

Figure 2-1. Directory tree

When you use the directory, you may be asked to enter the *path*. The path indicates how to get from where you are to the desired directory. For example, this is the path to a document called MYDOC.WPP. First C: identifies the drive. Then, a backslash (\) identifies the root. WP51 shows the software directory and then the name of the document follows. The directory and document name are separated by a backslash.

`C:\WP51\MYDOC.WPP`

Network Notes

Installing WordPerfect on a network is usually considered a fairly advanced task. WordPerfect walks you through installing the server, the primary computer with the hard disk to which other computers are attached. It also helps you install the computers, called *workstations*, that are hooked to the server. If you run into problems when you install, don't hesitate to seek help from your dealer or another knowledgeable source.

Using the Keyboard and Monitor

When you install WordPerfect, you will enter commands with your keyboard. You will simply type in words or letters and

15

press the Enter key. Sometimes you will be able to press the keys marked PgUp (page up) and PgDn (page down) to move through selections and then type in a letter or a number for the selection you desire.

How do you know what to type in? WordPerfect places text on your monitor screen that explains each step. During the installation process (and always when using any software) carefully read the messages on the screen. Sometimes these messages are called *prompts* since they prompt you on what to do. They typically tell you one or more of the following:

▶ What has happened
▶ What can happen (the options)
▶ The key(s) to press to do what you want
▶ The key(s) to press to stop what you are doing

16

Also pay attention to the lights on your computer and the noise. When your computer is working, the lights and sound are active. Typically, you must wait until the operation is done before you can proceed.

Using WordPerfect's Installation Process

To begin installing WordPerfect, place the WordPerfect disk with the word "Install" on the label in drive A of your computer. Type in this command

```
install
```

and press Enter.

A screen like that shown in Figure 2-2 appears. Now is the time to get in the good habit of carefully reading screens. You can see that to continue, you can press *y* for Yes. Anytime you see a letter in bright (bold) text, you can just press it to select the option instead of typing in the entire word.

After you have selected Yes to continue, WordPerfect attempts to identify whether you have a hard disk or floppy disk system. Enter the appropriate response (Yes or No) to this educated guess. Eventually, you will be taken to the Installation screen shown in Figure 2-3. Make your selection. For

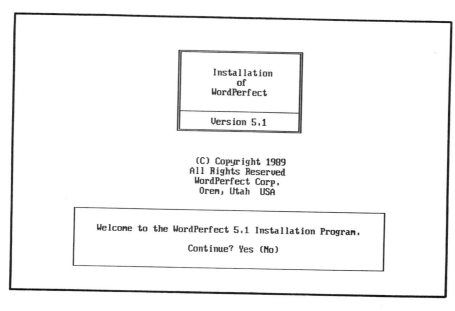

```
┌─────────────────────────────────┐
│         Installation            │
│              of                 │
│          WordPerfect            │
├─────────────────────────────────┤
│          Version 5.1            │
└─────────────────────────────────┘

        (C) Copyright 1989
        All Rights Reserved
        WordPerfect Corp.
        Orem, Utah  USA

┌─────────────────────────────────────────┐
│  Welcome to the WordPerfect 5.1 Installation Program. │
│                                         │
│          Continue? Yes (No)             │
└─────────────────────────────────────────┘
```

Figure 2-2. Installation welcome screen

example, if you are just getting started *and* are not working on a network, select 1 - Basic. If you are performing a special operation (for example, installing on a network), you may want to use another option, but the beginner's best approach is to keep it simple and use Basic.

After making your Installation screen selection, you are walked through a series of screens. WordPerfect tells you when to replace the disk in the drive with another disk. Note the name of the disk WordPerfect requests, find the disk with that label, and—when the drive light is off—place it in the drive.

> ⊘ **Caution:** Never remove or replace a disk in a drive when the drive light is on or you might damage the disk.

WordPerfect explains each feature as you install it. If you aren't sure that you want to install a particular feature, go ahead and select Yes to install it. Having features you don't use only takes up some space, but failing to install a feature you later want costs you time and causes confusion when you

```
Installation
    1 - Basic        Perform a standard installation (A:\ to C:\WP51).
                     New directories will be created if necessary.
                     Recommended for first-time installation.

    2 - Custom       Perform a customized installation.  (User selected
                     directories.)

    3 - Network      Perform a customized installation onto a network.
                     (To be performed by the network supervisor.)

    4 - Printer      Install updated Printer (.ALL) File.

    5 - Update       Install updated program file(s).

    6 - Copy Disks   Install every file from an installation diskette to a
                     specified location.  (Useful for installing all the
                     Printer (.ALL) Files.)




Selection: 3
```

Figure 2-3. Installation screen

18

have to install that feature alone. Plus, until you understand
WordPerfect, it is difficult to distinguish which features you
won't need. So, installing each feature early in your WordPerfect experience can only help you.

One of the final features you install is the link to your
printer. When you get to the printer screen, the operation is a
little more complex than just selecting Yes or No. The printer
screen is shown in Figure 2-4.

The printer screen lists all the printers WordPerfect will
work with. Find out the brand and model of your printer.
Then, press PgUp and PgDn until you see that printer and
model. Type in the number to the left of the printer name and
press Enter. This installs the files for that printer only. Continue following the messages.

If you can't find the brand or model of your printer, you
want to select the printer most like your own. Consult your
printer dealer or the dealer that sold you WordPerfect.

After selecting your printer, you'll come to a screen that
asks you to enter your registration number. This is a good idea
in case you need to use it when calling WordPerfect Corpora-

```
 1  Alphacom Alphapro 101
 2  Alps Allegro 24
 3  Alps ALQ200/300 (24 pin)
 4  Alps ALQ224e/324e
 5  Alps P2000
 6  Alps P2100
 7  Alps P2400C
 8  Apple LaserWriter IINTX
 9  Apple LaserWriter IINT
10  Apple LaserWriter Plus
11  Apple LaserWriter
12  AST TurboLaser
13  Brother HL-8e
14  Brother HR-15XL
15  Brother HR-20
16  Brother HR-35
17  Brother HR-40
18  Brother Twinriter 6
19  C.ITOH F10-40 Starwriter
20  C.ITOH F10-55 Printmaster
21  Canon BJ-130
22  Canon LBP 4

N Name Search;  PgDn More Printers;  PgUp Previous Screen;  F3 Help;
Selection: 0
```

19

Figure 2-4. Printer screen

tion for help. Take the time to find it and type it in when
asked.

Any special messages about your printer appear at the end
of the installation process. If your printer is attached and you
want to make a hard copy of the information for later reference, press the Shift key and the key marked PrtSc (print
screen) simultaneously. To use this function, your printer must
be linked to your computer by a cable, be turned on, be on line
(usually an on-line light is lit), and have paper in it.

When installation is done, this message appears:

Installation Complete.

To be safe, turn off your computer and then start it up again.
This way, any changes to the files will take affect.

> ▶ **Hint:** If you change printers later, you can use the
> installation procedure to install a new printer. From
> the Installation screen, select 4 - Printer. Select the new
> printer just like you did in Basic installation.

Once WordPerfect is installed, place the original disks from WordPerfect Corporation in a safe, temperate environment. These are your final backup copies so you don't want anything to happen to them.

Starting WordPerfect

Once WordPerfect is installed, you can start to use it.

On a two-drive system, make sure the computer is turned on and the WordPerfect disk is in drive A. From the A prompt, type in *wp* (for WordPerfect).

From a hard disk, type in *wp* at the DOS prompt. Or go to the WordPerfect directory by typing in the change directory (*cd*) command, followed by the path to the directory, and press Enter. For example, you could use this command line if you used the Basic installation:

20

```
cd\wp51
```

The advantage to starting from the WP51 directory is that you won't later have to change the directory when you save and retrieve files.

The screen shown in Figure 2-5 appears, followed by the screen shown in Figure 2-6. Don't be alarmed that very few messages appear. In the next chapter, you'll learn how to display the menu shown in Figure 2-7, from which you can select what you want.

Summary

In this chapter you've learned:

▶ You must format floppy disks to work with your computer.

▶ You must install WordPerfect to work with your computer. This is a one-time operation.

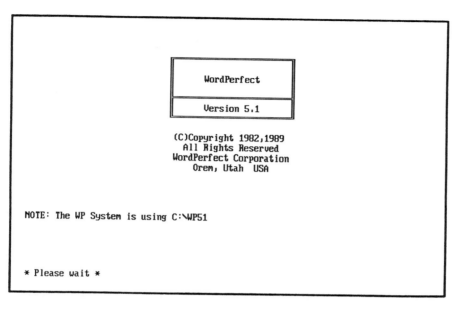

Figure 2-5. The first WordPerfect screen

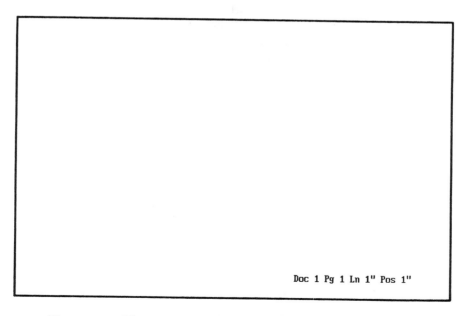

Figure 2-6. The next WordPerfect screen

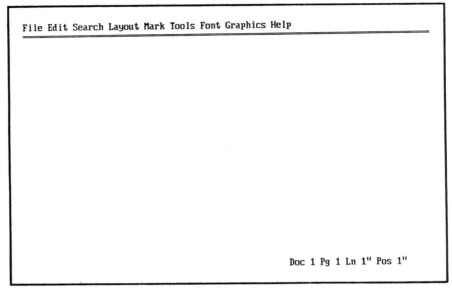

File Edit Search Layout Mark Tools Font Graphics Help

Doc 1 Pg 1 Ln 1" Pos 1"

Figure 2-7. The WordPerfect menu

► Use the Basic installation process to begin. Install all the features unless you are sure you don't need a particular feature.

► Start WordPerfect by typing in *wp* after the prompt for the drive where the WordPerfect files are stored.

Chapter 3

Getting Around with Menus, Keyboard, and Mouse

In This Chapter

▶ *The keys on the keyboard*
▶ *How to set up and use the mouse*
▶ *Making WordPerfect selections*
▶ *How to set up and use the menus*
▶ *How to use the keyboard to move the cursor*
▶ *Using the Help option*

The Keyboard

The keyboard lets you communicate with WordPerfect. The keys on the keyboard are shown in Figure 3-1.

A description of each group of keys follows. Find these on your own keyboard.

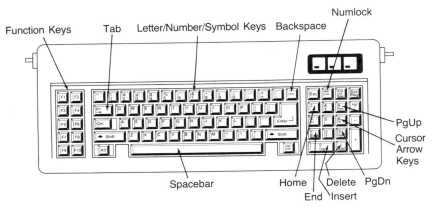

Figure 3-1. Keys on the keyboard

24

▶ The *Letter/Number/Symbol* keys are common to computers and typewriters. Press these to type in letters, numbers, and symbols. Press the *Shift* key to type in a capital letter or the symbol or punctuation mark on the top half of any other key.

▶ The *Function* keys are labeled F1 through F10 (F12 on some computers). They are used to perform special WordPerfect functions. They may be used alone or in conjunction with other keys including *Alt*, *Ctrl*, or Shift. This book uses the convention of hyphenating two key names, such as Shift-F1, to indicate you are to press the two keys simultaneously (the Shift key with the F1 key in this example).

▶ The *Cursor Arrow* keys are used to move the cursor. You can use the cursor arrow keys to move across existing text without changing the text. On most computers, pressing the key marked *Num Lock* first will produce the numbers on these keys instead of the arrows.

▶ The *Spacebar* is used to enter spaces or blank out text.

▶ The *Home*, *PgUp*, *End*, and *PgDn* keys are used for special WordPerfect movements.

▶ The *Tab*, *Backspace*, *Insert*, and *Delete* keys are used for special functions described later in this book.

The Mouse

If the only type of mouse that draws your attention is the furry variety, you can skip this section. It covers setting up and using the mechanical type of mouse with WordPerfect.

Setting Up the Mouse

Before you can use your mouse, you must introduce it to WordPerfect by type and connection. (Ask your mouse dealer to help you if you don't know the settings to make.)

To set up the mouse, select Shift-F1 Setup. The Setup menu appears. Select 1 - Mouse and the Setup: Mouse menu appears. Select 1 - Type and the Setup: Mouse Type menu, shown in Figure 3-2, appears.

25

```
Setup: Mouse Type

   IBM PS/2 Mouse
   Imsi Mouse, 2 button (Serial)
   Imsi Mouse, 3 button (Serial)
   Keytronic Mouse (Bus)
   Keytronic Mouse (Serial)
   Logitech Mouse (Bus)
   Logitech Mouse (Serial)
   Microsoft Mouse (Bus)
   Microsoft Mouse (Inport Bus)
 * Microsoft Mouse (Serial)
   Mouse Driver (MOUSE.COM)
   Mouse Systems Mouse, 3 button (Serial)
   MSC Technology PC Mouse 2 (Serial)
   Numonics Mouse (Serial)




 1 Select; 2 Auto-select; 3 Other Disk; N Name Search: 1
```

Figure 3-2. Setup: Mouse Type menu

Use the up and down cursor arrow keys to select the type of mouse you are using. When it is highlighted, press Enter. Return to the Mouse: Setup menu and check the 2 - Port setting, which refers to where the mouse is attached to your computer. If, according to what your mouse dealer told you, this is incorrect, select 2 - Port and change the setting. Press F7 Exit to return to your document screen. You know the mouse is properly set up when the pointer moves across the screen when you move the mouse on your desk.

Using a Mouse

The mouse pointer is the equivalent of the cursor. It marks your place on the screen. To use a mouse, simply move it across your desk. The roller on the bottom of the mouse causes the pointer to move across the screen. If you run out of desk space, just pick up the mouse and reposition it on the desk; the pointer position will remain unchanged on your screen.

Use the buttons on the top of the mouse to achieve the actions described by the special terms listed in Table 3-1.

Table 3-1. Mouse terms

Term	Mouse Action
Point	Place the mouse marker on a spot
Click	Press a button once
Double click	Press a button twice quickly
Drag	Press a button and hold it down while moving the mouse

The mouse can be used for movement on the screen and in setting Yes/No options. Table 3-2 describes each of those.

Table 3-2. Moving the mouse

Screen Movement	Mouse Action
Move the cursor to a spot	Point to the spot and press the left button
Move to parts of the document that are off the screen	Press and hold the right button, drag the mouse to the edge of the screen; release the button to stop the screen movement
Select Yes or No response	Point to the response and click

Making WordPerfect Selections

When you work with WordPerfect, you usually have two options for selecting WordPerfect functions. You can:

▶ Press a function key alone or in combination with the Alt, Ctrl, or Shift key.

▶ Make a menu selection with the keyboard or mouse. Read on to learn what a menu is and how to use WordPerfect's menu system to get fluent in WordPerfect quickly.

Menus

27

When you first enter WordPerfect, the screen resembles a blank stare. Most new users quite rightly don't know what to make of it. To get WordPerfect to give you a hint about what to do, you need to set up and use the menu system.

A menu on a computer screen is similar to a menu in a restaurant. Each offers a choice of options, but once you pick a selection on a computer menu, you are often presented with other options. For example, Figure 3-3 shows the initial menu, called the *main* WordPerfect *menu*. If you select File, the options for handling a file appear. The File menu is shown in Figure 3-4. The menus that appear from the main menu are called *pull-down* menus since the effect is that they are pulled down from the first selection. Notice that from the File menu, you can print, exit WordPerfect, or select any other option related to file handling.

Most of WordPerfect's menus are organized in a logical fashion. For example, to handle a file, just look at the File menu. Initially, you may forget which menu to look at and find yourself cruising through the menus to find a particular option. Don't worry about this. In time you will remember more and more menu/option combinations.

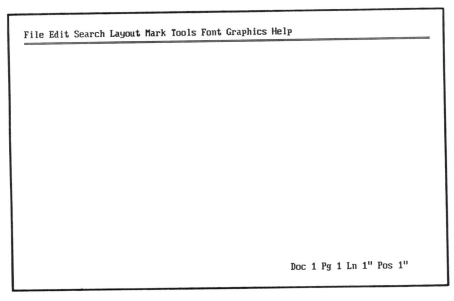

File Edit Search Layout Mark Tools Font Graphics Help

Doc 1 Pg 1 Ln 1" Pos 1"

Figure 3-3. WordPerfect menu

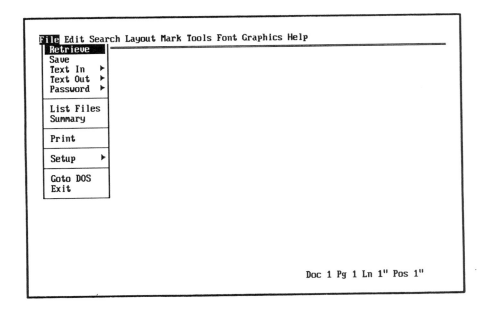

File Edit Search Layout Mark Tools Font Graphics Help

Retrieve
Save
Text In   ▶
Text Out   ▶
Password   ▶

List Files
Summary

Print

Setup   ▶

Goto DOS
Exit

Doc 1 Pg 1 Ln 1" Pos 1"

Figure 3-4. File menu

Setting Up the Menu

In WordPerfect's initial setting, the menu does not appear.
You'll probably want to change this so that the menu always
appears. You can later change back if you like.

To cause the menu to always appear, press Shift-F1 Setup.
The Setup menu shown in Figure 3-5 appears. Select 2 Display. The Setup: Display menu, shown in Figure 3-6, appears.

```
Setup

     1 - Mouse

     2 - Display

     3 - Environment

     4 - Initial Settings

     5 - Keyboard Layout

     6 - Location of Files




Selection: 0
```

Figure 3-5. Setup menu

On the Setup: Menu Options menu, make these selections
and press *y* to set each at Yes:

4 - Alt Key Selects Pull-Down Menu: Once you select Yes,
you may press the Alt key to go to the menu.
7 - Menu Bar Separator Line: When you select Yes, a line
divides the menu from the document, making it easier to
distinguish menu from document.
8 - Menu Bar Remains Visible: When you select Yes, the
menu will remain visible every time you use WordPerfect.

Once you have these set appropriately, Yes should appear for
each option.

```
Setup: Display

        1 - Colors/Fonts/Attributes

        2 - Graphics Screen Type        None Selected

        3 - Text Screen Type            Auto Selected

        4 - Menu Options

        5 - View-Document Options

        6 - Edit-Screen Options




    Selection: 0
```

30

Figure 3-6. Setup: Display menu

To make menu selections, you can type in the letter that is highlighted in bold or underlined. (You may need to adjust your screen to see which letter is highlighted.) If the Setup: Menu Options menu appears with a letter in each selection clearly brighter (bolded), you may leave "as is" the other options on this menu. For example, the M on 1 - Menu Letter Display should be bold. If you want, you can underline all the letters that are otherwise bold. Figure 3-7 illustrates the main menu and the File menu with the letters underlined just to give you an idea of this look.

To underline the letters, select and change the setting for each of these options on the Setup: Menu Options menu:

> *1 - Menu Letter Display*: To change letter appearance on full-screen menus like the Setup: Menu Options menu.
> *3 - Pull-Down Letter Display*: To change letter appearance on the pull-down menus from the WordPerfect menu.
> *5 - Menu Bar Letter Display*: This affects the letter appearance on the main WordPerfect menu.

Once you make any of these selections, this message appears:

1 Size; 2 Appearance; 3 Normal:

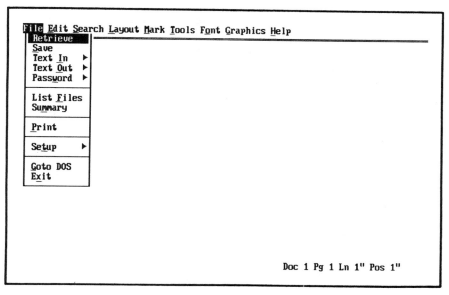

Figure 3-7. Menu letters underlined

Select 2 Appearance and this message appears:

1 Bold 2 Undln 3 Dbl Und 4 Italic 5 Outln 6 Shadw 7 Sm Cap 8 Redln
9 Stkout:

Select 2 Undln for each option on which you want the letter to
appear underlined.

Once you have completed all the work on the Setup:
Menu Options menu, press F7 Exit until you are returned to
the main WordPerfect menu. The menu appears according to
your settings.

Using the Menu

To make a menu selection from your keyboard, press the Alt
key to go to the menu. Your cursor goes to the menu and File
is highlighted. Next, press the left or right arrow keys until the
option you want is highlighted. Press Enter to pull down the
menu or type in the bold or underlined letter of the menu
selection to pull down the menu. When you are ready to leave
the menu and return to your document, press Esc.

31

To use a mouse, move it on your desk until the pointer is over the selection you want. Click the left mouse button to pull down the menu. To make menu selections, use the left mouse button. To exit from a menu, use the right mouse button. If you double click the left mouse button it is the same as pressing the left mouse button and then pressing Enter. If you often find yourself clicking the left button and then pressing Enter, you can save steps by double clicking. If you press the right mouse button with the menu displayed, it will hide the menu. Click it again to make the menu visible again.

Table 3-3 summarizes the ways to use the menu.

Table 3-3. Using menus

Action Desired	How to Perform
To access the menu line	Press Alt
To pull down a menu	▶Highlight with the left or right cursor arrow keys and press Enter ▶Press the bold or underlined letter of the menu ▶Point with the mouse and click the left button
To leave a menu	Press Esc as necessary or click the right mouse button

Using the Keyboard to Move the Cursor

As you enter text, the cursor moves to mark your place. When you come to the end of a line, don't press Enter. Just keep typing and the cursor "wraps around" at the line's end. This is Word-Perfect's wrap-around feature. When you later edit the text in the line, the line, as changed, also wraps around within the margins. For example, in Figure 3-8 the end of the first line of the letter wraps around at the appropriate spot. When the line is changed (see Figure 3-9) the line still wraps around.

Some keyboard actions allow you to move the cursor quickly. These are called quick movement keys. Table 3-4 summarizes the quick movement keys. Refer to it as you begin working in WordPerfect.

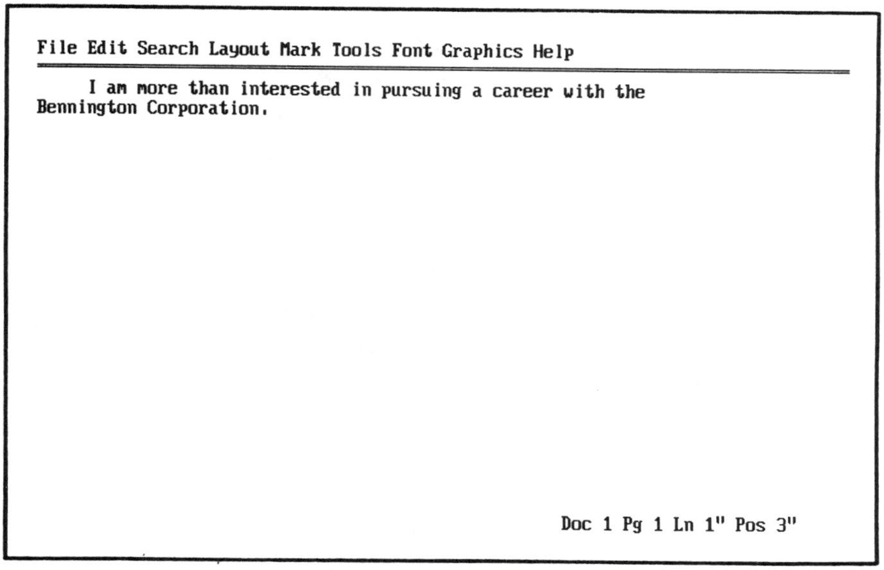

```
File Edit Search Layout Mark Tools Font Graphics Help
─────────────────────────────────────────────────────────
     I am more than interested in pursuing a career with the
Bennington Corporation.




                                         Doc 1 Pg 1 Ln 1" Pos 3"
```

33

Figure 3-8. Line wraps around before editing

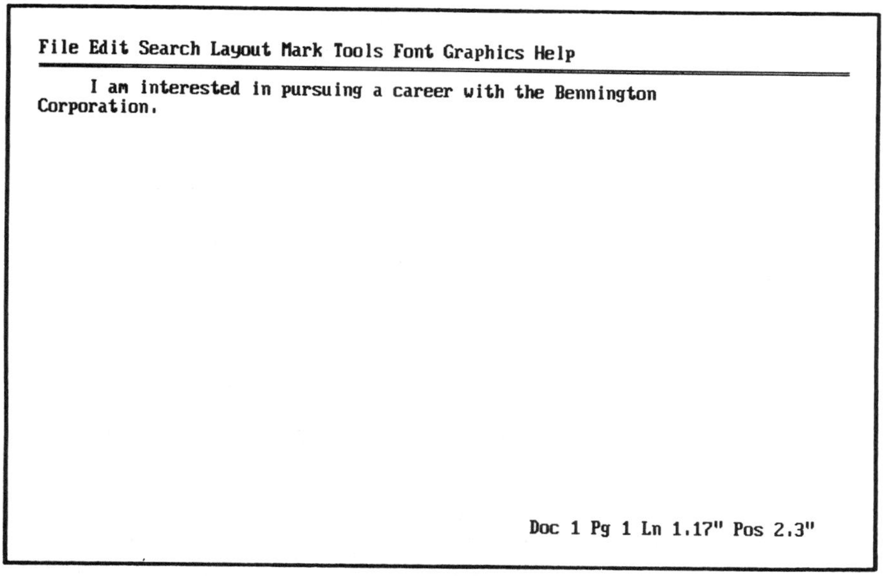

```
File Edit Search Layout Mark Tools Font Graphics Help
─────────────────────────────────────────────────────────
     I am interested in pursuing a career with the Bennington
Corporation.




                                       Doc 1 Pg 1 Ln 1.17" Pos 2.3"
```

Figure 3-9. Line wraps around after editing

Table 3-4. Quick movement keys

Action	Keys to Press
Move one character left	Left cursor arrow
Move one character right	Right cursor arrow
Left a word	Ctrl with left arrow (Word Left)
Right a word	Ctrl with right arrow (Word Right)
Left edge of screen	Home, then left arrow
Right edge of screen	Home, then right arrow
Left of line (even beyond screen)	Home, Home, left arrow
Right of line (even beyond screen)	Home, Home, right arrow
Up a single line	Up arrow
Down a single line	Down arrow
Top of the screen	Home, then up arrow
Bottom of the screen	Home, then down arrow
First line on previous page	PgUp
First line on next page	PgDn
Up a paragraph	Ctrl, then up arrow
Down a paragraph	Ctrl, then down arrow
Beginning of document (after WordPerfect codes)	Home, Home, up arrow
Beginning of document (before WordPerfect codes)	Home, Home, Home, up
End of document (before WordPerfect codes)	Home, Home, down arrow or Home, Home, Home, down arrow
Go to a character or page number you type in	Ctrl-Home

The status line appears on the last line of the screen. On the right, this appears:

Doc 1 Pg 1 Ln 2" Pos 3"

This information indicates which of two possible WordPerfect documents you are working with. Then, information about your cursor position appears. Shown are the page (Pg) number, the line (Ln) position in inches from the top of your page, and the position (Pos) in inches from the left of the page. Messages about WordPerfect operations also appear at the bottom of your screen. So, keep an eye on what's happening down there.

Help!

WordPerfect can answer your cry of Help! Just select Help on the menu. You have three options from which to choose:

▶ *Help*: This leads you to a screen for an alphabetical list of features or you can press a function key to get information about that key.
▶ *Index*: This option shows you an index of keys, features, and keystrokes.
▶ *Template*: This illustrates the template for the function keys on an IBM keyboard.

35

Take some time to play with the Help feature. It can answer your questions and save you some frustrating moments.

Summary

In this chapter you've learned:

▶ Each key on the keyboard has a different use.
▶ You must set up the mouse before using it. Pointing, dragging, and clicking the mouse buttons can produce different results.
▶ You may make WordPerfect selections with the keyboard or mouse.
▶ You must set up menus before you can use them.
▶ You have a variety of options for moving the cursor with the keyboard.
▶ Select Help from the menu to use the available Help options.

Chapter 4

Working with Words

In This Chapter

- ▶ *The codes placed in your document and how to view them*
- ▶ *How to insert text*
- ▶ *How to type over text*
- ▶ *How to use the Thesaurus*
- ▶ *How to automatically hyphenate text*

Codes in Your Document

As you work in WordPerfect, certain actions affect the text on your screen. For example, when you press the Tab key, a tab is inserted. Some word processors put codes on the screen to symbolize which action is affecting text. Having all these codes among your text can get confusing. WordPerfect leaves your text pretty much in a "what you see is what you get" state, even though codes are still placed in your text and can be seen through the Reveal Codes screen. The benefits of this approach are:

▶ Omission of confusing symbols on your screen

▶ Longer codes (instead of cryptic symbols) can be used, which fully explain the action taken

To see the codes, press Alt-F3 Reveal Codes or select Reveal Codes on the Edit menu. The Reveal Codes screen appears on the bottom half of your screen. It not only shows the text in the document but also each code entered.

Let's look at an example. The address entered for a letter, along with the Reveal Codes screen, are shown in Figure 4-1. When the Reveal Codes screen is active, the regular document text is shown at the top of the screen. The same text with the codes appears at the bottom of the screen after the triangle shapes. Notice these codes:

[HRt]
[Tab]
[SRt]

38

The [HRt] code stands for a "hard return." This shows each place you have pressed the Return or Enter key. The [Tab] code shows where the Tab key was entered. The [SRt] codes stands for "soft return." This code is automatically entered by WordPerfect and shows where each line wraps around.

```
File Edit Search Layout Mark Tools Font Graphics Help
─────────────────────────────────────────────────────────
Mr. David Randolph
Vice President
Bennington Corporation
45 Superstition Highway
Phoenix, Arizona 85251

Dear Mr. Randolph:

     I am interested in pursuing a career with the Bennington
                              Doc 1 Pg 1 Ln 1" Pos 2.8"
[   ▲   ▲   ▲   ▲   ▲   ▲   ↲   ▲   ▲   ▲   ▲   ▲   }   ▲   ▲
Mr. David Randolph[HRt]
Vice President[HRt]
Bennington Corporation[HRt]
45 Superstition Highway[HRt]
Phoenix, Arizona 85251[HRt]
[HRt]
Dear Mr. Randolph:[HRt]
[HRt]
[Tab]I am interested in pursuing a career with the Bennington[SRt]
Corporation.

Press Reveal Codes to restore screen
```

Figure 4-1. Address and Reveal Codes screen

You should use the Reveal Codes screen when you want to insert, move, or copy text. This way, you can make sure the code is handled properly along with the text. Also, if your text looks odd, you may have entered a code inadvertently. Just check the Reveal Codes screen and remove any unwanted codes.

Insert and Typeover Text

When you type in text, it is inserted among existing text. This is called working in *insert mode*. It is WordPerfect's default. In insert mode, the text to the right of your cursor moves right to make room for the new text. For example, in the letter shown in Figure 4-2, the phrase "As I mentioned in our conversation today," was inserted after the tab and before the beginning of the existing sentence. That sentence moved to the right and wrapped around automatically.

39

```
File Edit Search Layout Mark Tools Font Graphics Help

Mr. David Randolph
Vice President
Bennington Corporation
45 Superstition Highway
Phoenix, Arizona 85251

Dear Mr. Randolph:

     As I mentioned in our conversation today, I am interested in
pursuing a career with the Bennington Corporation.




                                        Doc 1 Pg 1 Ln 2.5" Pos 6"
```

Figure 4-2. Insert mode

WordPerfect also allows you to type over existing text rather than inserting text. You may go into *typeover mode*, which means any characters you type will replace existing characters. Take a look at the letter in Figure 4-3. The word "mentioned" in "As I mentioned" was typed over with the word "discussed." Notice that the word "Typeover" appears at the bottom left of the screen. This replaces the path and document name every time you are in typeover mode.

40

```
File Edit Search Layout Mark Tools Font Graphics Help
─────────────────────────────────────────────────────────

Mr. David Randolph
Vice President
Bennington Corporation
45 Superstition Highway
Phoenix, Arizona 85251

Dear Mr. Randolph:

      As I discussed in our conversation today, I am interested in
pursuing a career with the Bennington Corporation.




Typeover                                    Doc 1 Pg 1 Ln 2.33" Pos 2.9"
```

Figure 4-3. Typeover mode

To switch between insert mode and typeover mode, just press the Insert key (marked Ins on most computers). This key is called a "toggle" key since pressing it toggles you between one option and another.

Thesaurus

WordPerfect's Thesaurus is simple to use and often overlooked. When you say "that's not quite the word I want," call up WordPerfect's Thesaurus for other suggestions.

To use the Thesaurus, place your cursor on the word you want to look up. Press Alt-F1 Thesaurus or select Thesaurus from the Tools menu. (If you are using two disk drives, you may need to replace your WordPerfect program disk with your

Thesaurus disk.) Once you've asked for the Thesaurus, a screenful of suggestions appears. Figure 4-4 shows possible substitutions for the word "discussed." The document text appears at the top of the screen, followed by suggested words, and finally the bottom line shows the options. These options are:

> *1 Replace Word:* When you select 1 Replace Word, the message "Press letter for word" appears. Press the letter before the suggested word and that word replaces the word marked by the cursor in your document.
>
> *2 View Doc:* Select 2 View Document in order to scroll your document. This is especially helpful if you want to see the full context for the word you are replacing. The message "View: Press Exit when done" appears. Just press F7 Exit to go back to the Thesaurus screen.
>
> *3 Look Up Word:* If you think of a better word to look up, select 3 Look Up Word. The prompt Word: appears. Type in your word and press Enter. Suggested substitutions for that word appear.
>
> *4 Clear Column:* As you work in the Thesaurus, you may look up several words and not only fill all the columns but replace earlier columns of words with later columns of words. Select 4 Clear Column to move "back" to earlier columns.

41

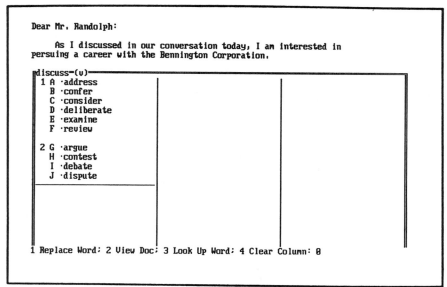

Figure 4-4. Thesaurus in action

Another option, which is not prompted on the screen, is available. That is the WordPerfect option to use when you want to stop an operation: Press F7 Exit to leave. When you do this from the Thesaurus, you are returned to your document without substituting a word.

▶ **Hint:** If you fool the Thesaurus with a word it does not recognize, WordPerfect tells you "Word not found" and allows you to enter a word.

Q **Using the Thesaurus**

1. Place your cursor on the word to look up and press Alt-F1 Thesaurus or select Thesaurus from the Tools menu.

   Suggested replacements for the word appear.

2. Select one of the options shown at the bottom of the screen to (1) replace the word, (2) view the document, (3) look up a new word, or (4) clear a column.

   Prompts for the selected operation appear. Follow the prompts to complete the operation.

42

Hyphenation

Some WordPerfect users like hyphenating words at the end of a line for more of an even right edge. Other users don't care and regard hyphenation as unnecessary. If you like hyphenating words, read on.

WordPerfect is smart enough to automatically hyphenate words for you; you simply turn hyphenation on. To do this, place your cursor where you want hyphenation to begin. Press Shift-F8 Format and then 1 Line (by typing a *1*) or select Line from the Layout menu. On the Format: Line menu, select 1

Hyphenation. Enter *y* to turn hyphenation on. To return to your document, press F7 Exit. The code [Hyph On] is placed in your text at the cursor location. The text you enter following the code will be hyphenated at the end of a line, if appropriate. If you later edit the text so the hyphenated words do not appear at the end of a line, the hyphenation stays in place but does not appear on your screen. This hyphen is called a "soft hyphen" because it only appears when the word is at the end of a line. You can always view the soft hyphen through the Reveal Codes screen.

Figure 4-5 shows our letter with hyphenation on. Notice that the Reveal Codes screen shows the [Hyph On] code before "Mr. David Randolph." Also notice that the word "very" was added and the word "interested" was hyphenated at the end of the line.

43

```
File Edit Search Layout Mark Tools Font Graphics Help

Mr. David Randolph
Vice President
Bennington Corporation
45 Superstition Highway
Phoenix, Arizona 85251

Dear Mr. Randolph:

     As I discussed in our conversation today, I am very interest-
                                        Doc 1 Pg 1 Ln 1" Pos 2.8"
[     ▲    ▲    ▲    ▲    ▲    ▲    ▲    ▲    ▲    ▲    ▲    }    ▲    ▲
[Hyph On]Mr. David Randolph[HRt]
Vice President[HRt]
Bennington Corporation[HRt]
45 Superstition Highway[HRt]
Phoenix, Arizona 85251[HRt]
[HRt]
Dear Mr. Randolph:[HRt]
[HRt]
[Tab]As I discussed in our conversation today, I am very interest-
ed in pursuing a career with the Bennington Corporation.[HRt]

Press Reveal Codes to restore screen
```

Figure 4-5. Hyphenation

To get rid of automatic hyphenation, you can turn hyphenation off by typing *n* for Hyphenation on the Line menu or you can delete the [Hyph On] code. You can delete hyphens already in place.

Ⓠ Automatic Hyphenation

1. Place your cursor where you want hyphenation to begin. Press Shift-F8 Format, then select 1 Line, or select Line from the Layout menu.

   The Format: Line menu appears.

2. Select 1 Hyphenation and press *y* to turn on hyphenation or *n* to turn it off.

   The selection is made.

3. Press F7 Exit until you return to your document.

   The hyphenation code is embedded in your document. ☐

44

If WordPerfect hyphenates a word that you don't want hyphenated, you can cancel the hyphenation. Place your cursor on the beginning of the word. Press Home and type in a slash. The code [/] appears in your document. Now delete the hyphen.

> ⊘ **Caution:** You can type in a hyphen with the hyphen (or minus) key. The hyphen will be in place even if you edit your document, however, and it may no longer be at the end of a line. This is not good. A preferable course is to use a soft hyphen (like the one WordPerfect inserts) which will "disappear" when the word is no longer at the end of a line. To do this, hold down Ctrl and type in a hyphen. The hyphen only appears on your screen when the word is at the end of a line.

For Your Information

When you set hyphenation from the Format: Line menu, you may have seen another hyphenation option: 2 Hyphenation Zone. The hyphenation zone is rarely used by beginning WordPerfect users (or many advanced users for that matter). It is a difficult concept and I'll try to put it as simply as possible. The hyphenation zone is the area WordPerfect uses to identify the valid region where a hyphen can occur. If you want more hyphens and a smoother right edge to your text or fewer hyphens and a more ragged edge, you can mess with the hyphenation zone. Check your WordPerfect manual if you think you'd like to change the settings.

Summary

In this chapter you've learned:

▶ Codes are placed in your document for many actions. You can view them through the Reveal Codes screen. Access this screen with Alt-F3 Reveal Codes, or, on extended keyboards, F11, or by selecting Reveal Codes on the Edit menu.

▶ You can use the Ins key to toggle between insert mode and typeover mode. In insert mode, text you type is inserted in existing text at your cursor location. In typeover mode, the text you type replaces existing text.

▶ To use the Thesaurus, place your cursor on the word you wish to look up. Press Alt-F1 Thesaurus or select Thesaurus from the Tools menu. Then select an option at the bottom of the screen.

▶ To control automatic hyphenation, press Shift-F8 Format then select 1 Line or select Line from the Layout menu. Select hyphenation and enter *y* or *n* to set your hyphenation choice.

45

Chapter 5

Deleting, Copying, and Moving Text

In This Chapter

▶ *How to delete text and cancel deletions (undelete)*
▶ *How to block text for manipulation*
▶ *How to move and copy text in a document*
▶ *How to retrieve moved or copied text*
▶ *How to append text*

Deleting Text

When you delete text, it is removed from the document. Because WordPerfect text may contain codes as well as text and spaces, it is a good idea to consult the Reveal Codes screen (Alt-F3) when you delete. This way you can be assured that you're deleting precisely the text, spaces, or codes you want to delete.

One way to get rid of text one character at a time is to press the Backspace key; the character, space, or code to the

left of the cursor is deleted as the cursor moves left. Figure
5-1a shows the "before" and Figure 5-1b, the "after" of pressing the Backspace key. Notice that the cursor is after the zip
code. After pressing Backspace once, the last number of the zip
code is deleted. On many computers, you can hold down the
Backspace key to continue deleting text until you release
the key.

```
File Edit Search Layout Mark Tools Font Graphics Help

Mr. David Randolph
Vice President
Bennington Corporation
45 Superstition Highway
Phoenix, Arizona 85251_

Dear Mr. Randolph:

     As I discussed in our conversation today, I am very interest-
ed in pursuing a career with the Bennington Corporation.

                                   Doc 1 Pg 1 Ln 1.67" Pos 3.2"
```

```
File Edit Search Layout Mark Tools Font Graphics Help

Mr. David Randolph
Vice President
Bennington Corporation
45 Superstition Highway
Phoenix, Arizona 8525_

Dear Mr. Randolph:

     As I discussed in our conversation today, I am very interest-
ed in pursuing a career with the Bennington Corporation.

                                   Doc 1 Pg 1 Ln 1.67" Pos 3.1"
```

Figure 5-1. (a) Backspace "before" (b) "After" backspace

Another way to delete text is to use the Delete key,
marked Del on many computers. Press Delete and the character, space, or code the cursor is on is deleted and all remaining
text on the page moves one position to the left. Figure 5-2a

illustrates text before Delete is pressed and Figure 5-2b, after Delete is pressed. The cursor is on the space before the "i" in "in our conversation today." Delete is pressed repeatedly until the rest of the phrase is deleted. Notice that the cursor remains in the same screen position. The text moves left and wraps around.

```
File Edit Search Layout Mark Tools Font Graphics Help

Mr. David Randolph
Vice President
Bennington Corporation
45 Superstition Highway
Phoenix, Arizona 85252

Dear Mr. Randolph:

     As I discussed_in our conversation today, I am very interest-
ed in pursuing a career with the Bennington Corporation.


                         Doc 1 Pg 1 Ln 2.33" Pos 3"
```

49

```
File Edit Search Layout Mark Tools Font Graphics Help

Mr. David Randolph
Vice President
Bennington Corporation
45 Superstition Highway
Phoenix, Arizona 85252

Dear Mr. Randolph:

     As I discussed, I am very interested in pursuing a career with
the Bennington Corporation.


                         Doc 1 Pg 1 Ln 2.5" Pos 3.7"
```

Figure 5-2. (a) "Before" pressing Delete (b) "After" pressing Delete

As with the Backspace key, on most computers holding down the Delete key repeats the delete. Your cursor stays in position and the text to the right of the cursor moves to the left as you delete one character at a time.

Deleting a Sentence, Paragraph, or Page

You may delete a sentence, a paragraph, or a page quickly with WordPerfect. The key to use is a little misleading because it is called *Move*. Bear with me . . . soon we will get to the delete option buried behind this key.

Put your cursor anywhere on the sentence, paragraph, or page you wish to delete. Then, press Ctrl-F4 Move or choose Select from the Edit menu. You will see this prompt:

```
Move: 1 Sentence; 2 Paragraph; 3 Page; 4 Retrieve
```

Enter the number that identifies the amount of text you want to delete.

As an example, suppose you aren't sure about David Randolph's actual title. Figure 5-3 illustrates the paragraph, in this

```
File Edit Search Layout Mark Tools Font [Graphics] Help

Mr. David Randolph
Vice President
Bennington Corporation
45 Superstition Highway
Phoenix, Arizona 85252

Dear Mr. Randolph:

     As I discussed, I am very interested in pursuing a career with
the Bennington Corporation.




Block on                                    Doc 1 Pg 1 Ln 1.17" Pos 2.4"
```

Figure 5-3. Highlighted paragraph for deletion

case, "Vice President," highlighted and ready for deletion. This prompt appears:

```
1 Move; 2 Copy; 3 Delete; 4 Append:
```

Press *3* for Delete. The highlighted text and spaces are deleted. These Quick Steps summarize the process.

Q Deleting a Sentence, Paragraph, or Page

1. Put the cursor on a sentence, paragraph, or page to delete.

   Your cursor marks the text.

2. Press Ctrl-F4 Move or pick Select on the Edit menu.

   The Move: prompt appears.

3. Select the amount of text to delete by pressing *1, 2,* or *3.*

   The sentence, paragraph, or page is highlighted. A prompt appears.

4. Select 3 Delete.

   The text is deleted.

51

Blocking Text

To delete, move, or copy larger blocks of text, you'll need to *block* the text. Blocking text marks the characters, spaces, and codes you want to manipulate. You must immediately perform the delete, move, or copy once you block text. Blocking text is also used to perform other functions such as centering a large amount of text. You can block text using the keyboard or with a mouse.

Blocking Text with a Keyboard

To block text with your keyboard, place your cursor on the first character, space, or code in the block. Press Alt-F4 Block or select Block from the Edit menu. "Block on" blinks in the lower left corner of the document portion of the screen. [Block] appears in the Reveal Codes screen. Move the cursor to the last character of the block of text. The text in the block is high-lighted. Figure 5-4 shows the Reveal Codes screen when "Vice President" is blocked. Notice that [Block] appears before "Vice President."

```
File Edit Search Layout Mark Tools Font [Graphics] Help

Mr. David Randolph
Vice President
Bennington Corporation
45 Superstition Highway
Phoenix, Arizona 85252

Dear Mr. Randolph:

     As I discussed, I am very interested in pursuing a career with
Block on                              Doc 1 Pg 1 Ln 1.33" Pos 1"
[   ▲   ▲   ▲   ▲   ▲   ▲   ▲   ▲   ▲   ▲   ▲   }   ▲   ▲
[Hyph On]Mr. David Randolph[HRt]
[Block]Vice President[HRt]
Bennington Corporation[HRt]
45 Superstition Highway[HRt]
Phoenix, Arizona 85252[HRt]
[HRt]
Dear Mr. Randolph:[HRt]
[HRt]
[Tab]As I discussed, I am very interest-ed in pursuing a career with[SRt]
the Bennington Corporation.[HRt]

Press Reveal Codes to restore screen
```

52

Figure 5-4. Blocked text

Now, when you perform the delete, copy, or move, the text is altered and then "Block on" disappears from the lower left of the screen. In our example, we are deleting the text, which involves a special prompt. After pressing delete, this message appears:

Delete Block? (Y/N)

Press *y* to delete the block. The result is shown in Figure 5-5. "Vice President" is deleted and since the cursor was after the return code at the end of the line, the code was deleted as well as the text.

 Blocking Text with the Keyboard

1. Put the cursor on the first character, space, or code in the block.	The cursor is in the character space.
2. Press Alt-F4 Block or select Block on the Edit menu.	**Block on** blinks in the lower left corner of the screen.

3. Move the cursor to the last character of the block of text.

The text is highlighted.

4. Perform the delete, copy, or move.

The text in the block is altered. If you are deleting, a message appears.

5. Press *y* to delete.

The block is deleted. ☐

If you press Alt-F4 to block text, then decide you don't want to block text, just press Alt-F4 again. "Block on" stops flashing and you may continue with other activities.

```
File Edit Search Layout Mark Tools Font Graphics Help

Mr. David Randolph
Bennington Corporation
45 Superstition Highway
Phoenix, Arizona 85252

Dear Mr. Randolph:

        As I discussed, I am very interested in pursuing a career with
the Bennington Corporation.
                                    Doc 1 Pg 1 Ln 1.17" Pos 1"
[   ▲   ▲   ▲   ▲   ▲   ▲   ▲   ▲   ▲   ▲   ▲   ▲   }   ▲   ▲
[Hyph On]Mr. David Randolph[HRt]
Bennington Corporation[HRt]
45 Superstition Highway[HRt]
Phoenix, Arizona 85252[HRt]
[HRt]
Dear Mr. Randolph:[HRt]
[HRt]
[Tab]As I discussed, I am very interest-ed in pursuing a career with[SRt]
the Bennington Corporation.[HRt]


Press Reveal Codes to restore screen
```

53

Figure 5-5. Result of deleting a block of text

Blocking Text with a Mouse

Blocking text with a mouse is as easy as pointing, dragging, and releasing. This feature is new to WordPerfect version 5.1.

Point to either end of the text to start highlighting. Press the left button and drag the mouse until the pointer is on the other end of the text to complete the block. Release the left button. The text is highlighted. The Reveal Codes screen shows the blocked text. Then delete, copy, or move text. A special warning prompt appears if you specify you want to delete the text.

Q Blocking Text with a Mouse

1. Point at one end of the text to highlight.	One end is identified.
2. Press the left button and drag the mouse to the other end of the text.	The text block is highlighted.
3. Release the left button.	The text is blocked.
4. Complete the operation. If you are deleting, respond to the special "Delete" message.	The blocked text is manipulated.

Canceling Deletions (Undelete)

With WordPerfect, you can afford an "oops" when you delete as long as you restore the text before making three other deletions. WordPerfect stores the most recent three deletions pretty much without regard to how small or large the deletion. To undo a deletion, put your cursor where you want the text to be restored. Press F1 Cancel or select Undelete from the Edit menu. When you cancel, you may select among the last three deletions and restore your selection. This message appears:

Undelete: 1 Restore; 2 Previous Deletion:

Continue to press *2* until the deletion you wish to restore appears. Then, press *1* to insert that deleted text.

If you happen to foil WordPerfect and make an unusually large deletion, WordPerfect will warn you:

Delete without saving for Undelete? (Y/N)

This message means you can go ahead and make your deletion, but it won't be available to be undeleted through F1 Cancel.

Some WordPerfect users like to employ the F1 Cancel option as a "quick and dirty" way to move or copy text. For example, you could delete the text you want to move or copy. Then you'd position the cursor in the first location to move or copy to. (If you are copying, you will copy the text back into its original position.) Press F1 Cancel to cancel the delete. Identify the text you want and restore it. Because a deletion is stored even after you have restored it, you may repeat a restoration as often as you like. This gives the effect of copying the text.

Moving Text

You may move a sentence, paragraph, page, or block of text at a time. When you move text, it is removed from the location you are moving from and is inserted in the location you are moving to. Figure 5-6 shows how text looks before and after the move: The last sentence and the second sentence have been transposed.

To move an unusual amount of text (not a complete sentence, paragraph, or page), block the text with F4 Block. The quickest way to move blocked text is to select Move from the Edit menu. Then, press Enter to insert the document at your cursor location.

A slower method to move text gives you the flexibility of either blocking or moving the text by sentence, paragraph, or page. To begin the move, press Ctrl-F4 Move or choose Select on the Edit menu. If you are moving a sentence, paragraph, or page, a prompt for Sentence, Paragraph, and Page appears. If you are moving a block, a Rectangle (a vertical block) or Block prompt is available so you can select the type of text you are moving. This prompt appears:

`1 Move; 2 Copy; 3 Delete; 4 Append:`

Select 1 Move. The highlighted text disappears from the screen. This prompt appears:

`Move cursor; press Enter to retrieve`

Place your cursor on the character before which the text should be inserted. (It's okay to edit text along the way; just don't

55

```
File Edit Search Layout Mark Tools Font Graphics Help
─────────────────────────────────────────────────────

Mr. David Randolph
Bennington Corporation
45 Superstition Highway
Phoenix, Arizona 85252

Dear Mr. Randolph:

        As I discussed, I am very interested in pursuing a career with
the Bennington Corporation.  I look forward to speaking with you
further on June 8th.  My complete resume is attached.




                                        Doc 1 Pg 1 Ln 2.67" Pos 1"
```

```
File Edit Search Layout Mark Tools Font Graphics Help
─────────────────────────────────────────────────────

Mr. David Randolph
Bennington Corporation
45 Superstition Highway
Phoenix, Arizona 85252

Dear Mr. Randolph:

        As I discussed, I am very interested in pursuing a career with
the Bennington Corporation.  My complete resume is attached.  I
look forward to speaking with you further on June 8th.




                                        Doc 1 Pg 1 Ln 2.33" Pos 3.7"
```

Figure 5-6. (a) Moved text before, and (b) After moving

press Enter until you are ready to retrieve the moved text.)
Press Enter.

Q Moving Text (Blocked or Not)

1. Block the text with Alt-F4 Block if necessary.	The blocked text is highlighted.
2. Press Ctrl-F4 Move or pick Select on the Edit menu.	Prompts appear according to the amount of text you are moving.
3. Select Sentence, Paragraph, Page, Block, or Rectangle.	A prompt with the Move option appears.
4. Select 1 Move.	The highlighted text disappears. A prompt appears.
5. Put the cursor where the text should go and press Enter.	The text is moved.

57

Copying Text

You may copy a sentence, a paragraph, a page, or a block of text. When text is copied, the original remains in place. A copy is stored by WordPerfect for you to retrieve at another spot in the document. Figure 5-7 illustrates a copy. From the inside address, "45 Superstition Highway" was copied into the sentence that has been added to the body of the letter.

The process for copying text is very similar to moving text. If you want to copy a block of text, highlight it with Alt-F4 Block. Select Copy from the Edit menu. With your cursor in the location where you want the text copied to, press Enter.

Like the move feature, you can copy by block, sentence, paragraph, or page with a longer process. Press Ctrl-F4 Move or choose Select on the Edit menu. One or more of these options appear: Sentence, Paragraph, Page, Rectangle, or Block.

Make your selection. This prompt appears:

1 Move; 2 Copy; 3 Delete; 4 Append

Select 2 Copy. The highlighted text remains on the screen. This prompt appears:

`Move cursor; press Enter to retrieve`

Place your cursor on the character before which the text should be inserted. You may edit text along the way. Don't press Enter until you are ready to retrieve the text. Once you are ready, press Enter. The text is inserted before the character that your cursor marks.

```
File Edit Search Layout Mark Tools Font Graphics Help
_____

Mr. David Randolph
Bennington Corporation
45 Superstition Highway
Phoenix, Arizona 85252

Dear Mr. Randolph:

     As I discussed, I am very interested in pursuing a career with
the Bennington Corporation. My complete resume is attached. I
look forward to speaking with you further on June 8th. I'll meet
you at your corporate office location at 45 Superstition Highway.




                                    Doc 1 Pg 1 Ln 2.83" Pos 1"
```

Figure 5-7. Copying text

 Copying Text

1. Mark the block with Alt-F4 Block if desired.

   The block is highlighted.

2. Press Ctrl-F4 Move or pick Select on the Edit menu.

   A prompt appropriate to the amount of text you are copying appears.

3. Select from among
   1 Sentence, 2 Paragraph,
   3 Page, 4 Rectangle, or
   1 Block.

The copy prompt appears.

4. Select 2 Copy.

The highlighted text
remains on the screen.

5. Put your cursor in the spot
   to insert text and press
   Enter.

The text is copied.

Retrieving Text

WordPerfect stores only the most recent text you moved or copied so that it can be retrieved. However, you may retrieve that
text as many times as you want (or until you move or copy other
text to the same storage area).

59

    To retrieve the last text moved or copied, place your cur-
sor on the character before which the text should be inserted.
Press Ctrl-F4 Move and this prompt appears:

Move: 1 Sentence; 2 Paragraph; 3 Page; 4 Retrieve:

Select 4 Retrieve and this prompt appears:

Retrieve: 1 Block; 2 Tabular Column; 3 Rectangle

Select 1 Block for regular text. The last text moved or copied is
inserted to the left of the character marked by the cursor.
    A quicker way to retrieve text is to use the Edit menu.
Select Paste. The same Retrieve prompt appears and you may
select 1 Block for regular text.

Appending Text

Sometimes you may want to add the text to the end of a file on
a disk. This is called *appending*. For example, you might add the

example letter to a file containing all letters sent to this company.

To append a block of text, you block the text first. Whether working with a block of text or not, begin the append by pressing Ctrl-F4 Move. If you are appending a block, this prompt appears:

`Move: 1 Block; 2 Tabular Column; 3 Rectangle`

Otherwise this prompt appears:

`Move: 1 Sentence; 2 Paragraph; 3 Page; 4 Retrieve:`

Depending on what you are appending, select 1 Sentence, 2 Paragraph, 3 Page, or 1 Block. This prompt appears:

`1 Move; 2 Copy; 3 Delete; 4 Append`

Select 4 Append and this prompt appears:

`Append to:`

Type in the drive designation, the path if necessary, and the name of the document file to which you want to append the text. Press Enter and the portion of the document to append is added to the end of the named document.

If you are blocking text, you can use the pull-down menu shortcut. Just block the text with Alt-F4 Block. Then, from the Edit menu, select Append. Select to File, type the file path and name, and press Enter.

> ▶ **Hint:** If the document file name you enter doesn't exist, WordPerfect creates it. This is a slick way to create a new document to hold your appended work.

For Your Information

There are options available through the F4 Move function which were not explained in this chapter. These functions are outside the scope of a beginning book, but I thought you might be curious. The Tabular Column and Rectangle options are used to mark, then move or copy columns made with tabs or rectangular areas. Keep this in mind as you learn to work with tabs and columns. All the move functions apply to those options as well.

Summary

In this chapter you've learned:

▶ To delete text, you can use the Backspace key, Delete key, or the Ctrl-F4 Move function or choose Select from the Edit menu.

▶ You can cancel deletion using F1 Cancel. The effect is to undelete one of the last three deletions.

▶ Mark text for manipulation using Alt-F4 Block. A variety of WordPerfect functions may be applied to blocked text including move, delete, or copy.

▶ You can move, copy, or retrieve text by using the Ctrl-F4 Move function or by picking Select from the Edit menu.

▶ Append text to the end of a file via the Ctrl-F4 Move function or with the Edit menu's Select option.

61

Chapter 6

Save Before You Exit

In This Chapter

▶ *Why you must periodically save your work*
▶ *How to save your work*
▶ *How to give a document a name*
▶ *How to exit WordPerfect*
▶ *Why and how to back up your documents*

Why You Must Save Your Work

We're so used to paper documents it can be hard to adjust to using documents in another form. Imagining the contents of a file drawer of paper stored on a slim disk is difficult for many. The common way to make the transition from paper to magnetic media is to use both until disk storage alone feels comfortable. Even if you make paper copies of everything, you still have to develop the good habit of routinely saving your work. Over time, your need for security in paper will diminish.

Save your work or lose it. While dramatic, this states a plain fact. As you work on a document it is stored in RAM, which is only available as long as there is power to the computer. When the power is cut off (maybe accidentally), the contents of RAM are lost. Saving a document to a disk is mandatory to ensure the document will be available to you when you need it. Because accidents happen to disks too, saving a document to more than one disk is your insurance that the document will be available even if one disk is lost or damaged.

Nearly every computer user can tell you a story of working for hours or days on an important document and then having the worst happen—the document is lost. Usually, a new computer user will exercise sloppy saving habits until a significant piece of work is lost. The loss may be the result of a loose power cord or an electrical voltage drop, and so on. The pain of losing the work then causes the user to pay greater attention to saving. Avoid the one-act tragedy. Always take time to save your work.

Good Saving Habits

64

Develop these good habits:

▶ Periodically save your work as you go. That way, if the power to your computer fails, you will have a recent, complete version of your work. How often to save? Any time you have entered edits that are significant (and that you wouldn't want to lose), save your work. For some, this is every 15 minutes. For others, it is every hour. A good rule is: When in doubt, save it.

▶ Always save more than one copy of your document on more than one disk. Disks can be damaged or lost.

▶ Use WordPerfect automatic *backup* options. WordPerfect has options to automatically make copies of your most recent edits as you work. Using this function will give you additional options for recovering your work if an accident happens.

How to perform each of these good saving habits is covered in detail in the remainder of this chapter.

Naming a Document

When you save a document, the document must have a name so that you and WordPerfect can find it again.

Names may be up to eight characters long. If you enter a name longer than eight characters, WordPerfect automatically lops off the characters beyond eight. The eight-character name may be followed by a period and an extension of three characters, however. For example, this document is named MYDOC and has an extension of WPP. Its full name is MYDOC.WPP.

When naming a document, you may use:

Letters A through Z
Numbers 0 through 9
Many symbols, such as: ! @ # $ % ^ & ( ) - _ '

65

Some symbols, though, will result in an "Invalid" message or "File creation error" message. An asterisk, for example, will provoke such a message. If you get such a message, omit any unusual symbols and try again.

Each document must have a unique name. You can store the same document under more than one name. It's a good idea to give a document a name that suggests the use of the document. Here are some examples:

LETDAVE1.WPP—The first letter to Dave
LETDAVE2.WPP—The second letter to Dave
IBBRPTV1.WPP—IBB Report, Version 1
ME020890.WPP—Memo of 2/8/90

When it comes to using an extension, my advice is:

► Always use one
► Use the same extension for all WordPerfect documents you create

By using an extension unique to only your WordPerfect documents you will be able to identify WordPerfect documents when they are stored on a disk with documents created with other software. For example, a disk might contain these documents:

WPCHAP1.WPP—.WPP is used for a WordPerfect document
LETJACK.DOC—.DOC is used for a MultiMate document
CH1FIGS.WK1—.WK1 is used for a Lotus 1-2-3 document

Because consistent extensions are used, it is clear which software to use to view each document. If inconsistent extensions are used, you might have to try the document with several software programs just to figure out what the document is all about.

It's recommended that you use .WPP as your WordPerfect extension since (to my knowledge) this is not automatically assigned by any other popular software package. (That statement is good for at least one letter.) Don't use .DOC since several word processors use that extension.

66

Saving Your Work as You Go

Save your work as you work. Do it every time you have performed edits you would hate to lose. Most people save their work between every 15 minutes and every hour.

From the document, press F10 Save Text or select Save from the File menu. A message like the following appears. (The drive, path, and document name only appear if the document has already been saved or retrieved.) Type in the drive, path, and document name, if needed, and press Enter.

Document to be saved: C:/WP51/DOC/BELET.WPP

In this example, to save the letter to the Bennington Corporation, we use drive C, WP51 as the directory for WordPerfect version 5.1, DOC as the document subdirectory, and BELET.WPP as the document name.

If this is the first time you are saving the document, this message appears as the document is saved:

Saving C:/WP51/DOC/BELET.WPP

If the document had already existed on disk, this message would have appeared:

Replace: C:/WP51/DOC/BELET.WPP? No (Yes)

No is the default for mouse users. Click on No if that's your choice. If you get the "Replace" message, press *y* for Yes to replace the "old" version on disk. A similar message to this one appears as the document is saved:

Saving C:/WP51/DOC/BELET.WPP

Q Saving a Document

1. Press F10 Save or select Save on the File menu.

   A prompt appears for the document name.

2. Type the drive, path, and document name as necessary and press Enter. If a "Replace" message appears, press *y*.

   The document is saved.

67

Because a disk might get damaged, you will want to save your work to more than one disk. You can do this by swapping disks in the disk drive using this approach:

▶ Save the document
▶ Change the disk in the document disk drive
▶ Save the document again

Or, to save to a hard disk and then to a disk in a disk drive:

▶ Save the document
▶ Save the document again (changing the drive designation)

Save, Then Exit, or Work with Different Document

Instead of saving the document and continuing, you may save the document, and then:

▶ Leave the document and exit WordPerfect or

▶ Leave the document and work with a different document

From the document, press F7 Exit or select Exit from the File menu. This message appears:

Save document? Yes (No)

Press *y* to save the document. A message like this appears:

Document to be saved: C:\WP51\DOC\BELET.WPP

If the document has not been named, the drive, path, and name area will be blank. If necessary, type in these, and press Enter. If this is the first time you are saving the document, this message appears as the document is saved:

68

Saving C:/WP51/DOC/BELET.WPP

If the document already exists on disk, this message appears:

Replace: C:/WP51/DOC/BELET.WPP? No (Yes)

If you get the "Replace" message, press *y* for Yes to replace the "old" version on disk. This message appears as the document is saved:

Saving C:/WP51/DOC/BELET.WPP

Once the document is saved, a message like this appears:

Exit WP? No (Yes)

Press *n* (for No) to keep working in WordPerfect. Or, press *y* (for Yes) to quit using WordPerfect. If you press *n* in order to keep working in WordPerfect, the document is cleared from the screen and a clear screen is available for your use. If you press *y* in order to exit WordPerfect, you are returned to the operating system prompt (such as C>). From the prompt, you may use other software or turn off the computer.

Save and Exit or Work with Different Document

1. Press F7 Exit or select Exit from the File menu.

   This message appears: Save document? Yes (No)

2. To save the document, press *y* for Yes and enter the drive, path, and document name.

   A "Saving" or "Replace" message appears.

3. If you get the "Replace" message, press *y*.

   The "Saving" message appears.

4. Press *n* to stay in WordPerfect or *y* to quit using WordPerfect.

   The document is cleared or you are returned to the operating system prompt.

▶ **Caution:** *Never* turn off the machine while in WordPerfect. This can damage your document or WordPerfect software. Always use F7 Exit to leave WordPerfect. Only turn off your computer if you are at the operating system prompt.

69

Exiting without Saving a Document

Occasionally, you may not want to save a document. For example, you may want to lose the edits made since your last save, or you may not have changed the document. Skipping the save step saves time. But use it only if you want to lose any edits made since the last save.

You can use F7 Exit to leave a document without saving it. You are then given a choice of either exiting WordPerfect or to continue working in WordPerfect (with the existing document cleared).

Using Exit without Saving a Document

1. From the document, press F7 Exit.

   This message appears: Save document? Yes (No)

2. To skip saving the document, press *n* for No.

   A message like this appears: Exit WP? No (Yes)

3. Press *n* (for No) to clear the document and continue working in WordPerfect. Or press *y* (for Yes) to quit using WordPerfect.

   If you press *n* to keep working in WordPerfect, the document is cleared. If you press *y*, you are returned to the operating system prompt (such as C>). From the operating system prompt, you can use other software or turn off the computer.

70

Remember, to avoid damaging your document or WordPerfect software, always use F7 Exit to leave WordPerfect and return to the operating system prompt before turning off the computer.

Saving Part of a Document

You may save just a part of a document, if you wish. This is useful when you want to delete the rest of the document. It is also useful when you want to place part of a document in a new document with a unique name. The result is to create a new document made up of a portion of the existing document.

Use Alt-F4 Block to block the part of the document you want to save. Press F10 Save Text or select Save from the File menu. This message appears:

Block name:

Type in the name of the document, including any extension, and press Enter. (Include the drive and path designation, if necessary.) The blocked portion of the document is saved under the new name and you are returned to your document.

Using WordPerfect's Automatic Backup Options

Using F10 Save Text saves the complete document to the drive, path, and document name identified. But, to effectively protect your documents, you must remember to periodically press F10 Save Text. To provide additional protection for the forgetful, WordPerfect has an automatic backup option. (You will still want to use F10 Save Text often in order to save your entire document.) WordPerfect also has an automatic backup option for the last saved document.

Setting up and using the automatic backup options is a little complex so you may want to go slow in this part. The two automatic backup options serve very different functions:

▶ *Timed Document Backup*: The document on your screen is saved at the time intervals you specify. It is saved in a file called WP{WP}BK.1 (or WP{WP}BK.2 if you have a second document on the screen). Saving takes a few seconds. When you exit WordPerfect properly, the WP{WP}BK files are deleted. If the power is accidentally cut off, the WP{WP}BK files remain on your disk. When you start WordPerfect, you can rename and load the appropriate WP{WP}BK file to see how much WordPerfect saved for you.

▶ *Original Document Backup*: When you save a document using F10 Save Text or F7 Exit, the last disk version of the document is saved rather than replaced with the new version. The older version is placed in a file called "filename.BK!" where "filename" is the actual name of the document file. This option has nothing to do with saving your document as you work. It only preserves the "last saved" version of the document. Since this option gives you two versions of each document (the current and the last saved version), more space is consumed on your disk than when you save only one version.

71

Setting Up the Backup Options

To set up automatic backup options, press Shift-F1 Setup. The menu in Figure 6-1 appears. Select option 1, Backup. The screen in Figure 6-2 appears. Press 1 to set the timed backup. Your cursor goes to the "Timed Document Backup Yes/No" field. Press *y* (for Yes). The field appears as Yes, and your cursor goes to the "Minutes Between Backups" field. Enter the number of minutes between backups (15 is suggested) and press Enter. The number of minutes appears and your cursor goes back to the "Selection" field at the bottom of the screen. Press *2* to set the original document backup option. Your cursor goes to the "Original Document Backup" field. Press *y* for Yes. Yes is entered, and your cursor goes back to the "Selection" field. To go back to your document, press F7 Exit and you are returned to the document screen.

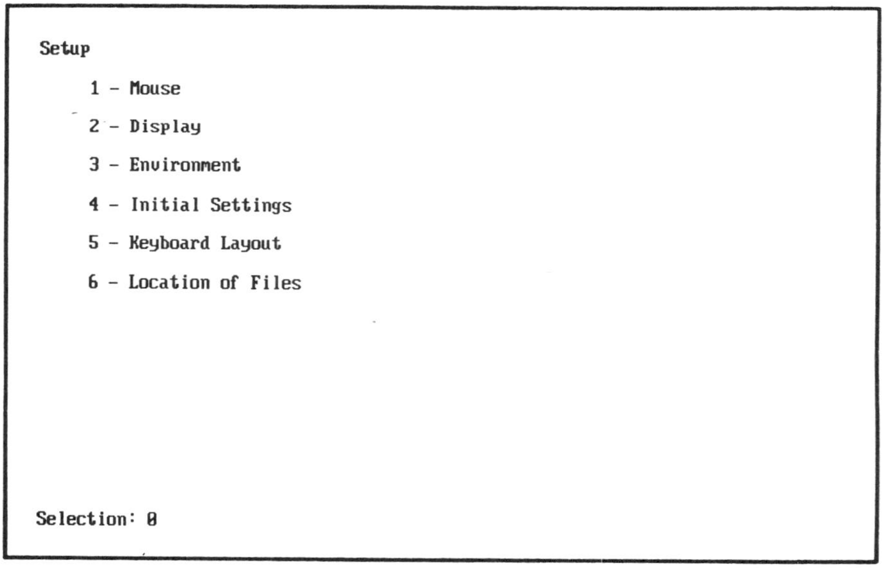

```
Setup

    1 - Mouse

    2 - Display

    3 - Environment

    4 - Initial Settings

    5 - Keyboard Layout

    6 - Location of Files






Selection: 0
```

Figure 6-1. Setup menu

Recovering After an Accident

If you set timed backup and have had the computer power fail, you will want to be able to recover the timed backup copy of your document. Before trying the recovery, make sure the prob-

```
Setup: Backup

        Timed backup files are deleted when you exit WP normally.  If you
        have a power or machine failure, you will find the backup file in the
        backup directory indicated in Setup: Location of Files.

            Backup Directory

    1 - Timed Document Backup                 Yes
            Minutes Between Backups           30


        Original backup will save the original document with a .BK! extension
        whenever you replace it during a Save or Exit.

    2 - Original Document Backup              No




Selection: 0
```

Figure 6-2. Automatic Backup Options screen

73

lem with the power supply is over. Then turn on your computer and start WordPerfect. A message like this appears:

`Old Backup File Exists. 1 Rename; 2 Delete:`

Press *1* to rename the WP{WP}BK file. A message to rename the file is displayed:

`New Name:`

Type in the file name and press Enter. (Don't give it the same name as the "old" file you were working with, in case the "old" file is a more complete copy. You may want to look at it later.) The backup file is renamed and WordPerfect is available for use.

You would now look at the contents of the timed backup file you renamed as well as the contents of the last version of the document you saved. Just like any other WordPerfect document, each document can be retrieved by using Shift-F10 Retrieve Text. Chapter 7 provides quick steps to retrieve documents in WordPerfect.

Summary

In this chapter you've learned:

- ▶ You must periodically save your work to protect your investment in time and effort in case of accidents.
- ▶ You can save your work using F10 Save Text or through F7 Exit.
- ▶ Document names may be up to eight characters in length, optionally followed by a period and three-character extension.
- ▶ *Always* exit WordPerfect using F7 Exit to avoid damage to your documents or to WordPerfect files.

74

Chapter 7

Ways to Retrieve a Document

In This Chapter

75

▶ *How to retrieve a document if you know the name*
▶ *How to retrieve a document if you don't remember the name*
▶ *How to look at but not retrieve a document*
▶ *How to change the designated drive and directory*
▶ *How to retrieve a document into another document*

Retrieving a Document

The term "retrieving a document" refers to moving the document from disk storage into RAM. Also referred to as "loading a document," you'll most often use the procedure when you wish to view the document, perhaps for editing.

Retrieving When You Know the Name

If speed is your goal, knowing its name when you want to retrieve a document is the fastest approach. Start from a "blank" WordPerfect screen. Press Shift-F10 Retrieve Text or select Retrieve from the File menu. This message appears:

`Document to be retrieved:`

Type in the drive and path, if necessary, along with the document name, including its extension. The text you enter may look something like this:

`Document to be retrieved:` C:\WP51\DOC\BELET.WPP

Here, C: shows the drive, WP51 and DOC are the directories, and BELET.WPP is the document name. The directory and document name are always set off by backslashes as shown here. Once you have identified the document, press Enter. The document appears on your screen.

76

Ⓠ Retrieving a Document When You Know Its Name

1. Press Shift-F10 Retrieve Text or select Retrieve from the File Menu.

   This message appears: `Document to be retrieved:`

2. Type in the path and document name, and then press Enter.

   The document is retrieved.

   ☐

After typing in the document name and pressing Enter, you may see a message like this:

`ERROR: File not found -- filename`

This means you have made a typographical error in the document drive, directory, or name; the information is incorrect; or the file does not exist on the disk. Whatever the reason, WordPerfect cannot match the information you provided with a document on the disk. If, after carefully checking your typing accuracy, you cannot determine the problem, it may be that you've forgotten the document name. In this event, use the following approach.

Retrieving When You Don't Know the Name

Sometimes you'll want to retrieve a document but not remember its name. Or, you'll attempt to retrieve a document by name and get a message like this:

ERROR: File not found BELET.WPP

In either case, you can consult WordPerfect for a list of document names and select a document from the list. To select from the list, you use cursor arrow keys or a mouse to highlight the desired document name.

Figure 7-1 shows an alphabetical list with the document BELET.WPP highlighted. The highlighted (or selected) document appears in a different color or in reverse video characters (usually light characters in a dark box). The drive and directory for these files appears at the top of the screen. Selections you can make are shown at the bottom of the screen and numbered.

```
01-01-80  12:35a           Directory C:\WP51\DOC\*.WPP
Document size:        0    Free: 14,325,760 Used:       665,278        Files:      63

    .    Current    <Dir>                   ..    Parent    <Dir>
1-5        .WPP        884  01-01-80 12:11a   BELET    .WPP        984  10-22-89 09:46p
BELET10E.WPP        1,533  10-29-89 10:05p   BELET111.WPP      2,062  01-01-80 12:53a
BELET112.WPP        1,081  01-01-80 07:11a   BELET41 .WPP        519  10-22-89 09:08a
BELET42 .WPP          561  10-22-89 09:11a   BELET45 .WPP        568  10-22-89 01:20p
BELET53 .WPP          788  10-28-89 02:20p   BELET76 .WPP        967  10-22-89 09:33p
BELET04 .WPP          984  10-22-89 09:45p   BENLET11.WPP        831  01-01-80 01:09a
WPF1     .WPP       13,707  10-28-89 03:18p   WPF1-50 .WPP     13,706  10-28-89 03:04p
WPF1-AS .WPP       12,541  10-28-89 03:05p   WPF10    .WPP     10,849  10-29-89 10:02p
WPF10-50.WPP       10,849  10-29-89 10:02p   WPF10-AS.WPP      9,553  10-29-89 10:03p
WPF11    .WPP       14,922  01-01-80 07:09a   WPF11-50.WPP     14,922  01-01-80 07:09a
WPF11-AS.WPP       13,659  01-01-80 07:10a   WPF12    .WPP     11,767  01-01-80 01:45p
WPF12-50.WPP       11,767  01-01-80 01:45p   WPF12-AS.WPP     10,566  01-01-80 01:46p
WPF13    .WPP       13,206  01-01-80 04:13a   WPF13-50.WPP     13,206  01-01-80 04:13a
WPF13-AS.WPP       11,973  01-01-80 04:14a   WPF14    .WPP     13,816  11-07-89 09:52p
WPF14-50.WPP       13,809  11-07-89 09:53p   WPF14-AS.WPP     10,139  11-07-89 09:54p
WPF15    .WPP       10,445  11-10-89 04:39p   WPF15-50.WPP     10,445  11-10-89 04:41p
WPF15-AS.WPP        9,357  11-10-89 04:41p   WPF2     .WPP     17,127  10-29-89 09:12a
WPF2-50 .WPP       17,127  10-29-89 09:13a ▼ WPF2-AS .WPP     15,809  10-29-89 09:14a

1 Retrieve; 2 Delete; 3 Move/Rename; 4 Print; 5 Short/Long Display;
6 Look; 7 Other Directory; 8 Copy; 9 Find; N Name Search: 6
```

Figure 7-1. List of documents with BELET.WPP highlighted

Selecting a name from a list is a useful way to retrieve a document when you have a lot of documents. It really is difficult to remember the exact spelling of each one when you have a lot of document names.

To retrieve a document when you don't know its name, press F5 List Files or select List Files from the File menu. A message like this appears:

```
Dir C: \WP51\DOC\*.*
```

This message displays the current drive; the path, if any; and *.* to indicate "all document names with document extensions." Type in the information WordPerfect will need to find the drive and directory for which you want to list documents. Keep the notation *.* in place of a document name. Press Enter. A screen appears showing the documents on your specified drive and directory. See Figure 7-2 for an example. Highlight the name of the document to retrieve and press 1 Retrieve. The document is retrieved.

78

```
01-01-80  12:35a              Directory C:\WP51\DOC\*.WPP
Document size:        0   Free: 14,325,760 Used:      665,278      Files:      63

   .   Current    <Dir>                    ..    Parent    <Dir>
1-5      .WPP        884   01-01-80 12:11a   BELET    .WPP        984  10-22-89 09:46p
BELET10E.WPP       1,533   10-29-89 10:05p   BELET111.WPP       2,062  01-01-80 12:53a
BELET112.WPP       1,081   01-01-80 07:11a   BELET41 .WPP        519   10-22-89 09:08a
BELET42 .WPP         561   10-22-89 09:11a   BELET45 .WPP        568   10-22-89 01:20p
BELET53 .WPP         788   10-28-89 02:20p   BELET76 .WPP        967   10-22-89 09:33p
BELET04 .WPP         984   10-22-89 09:45p   BENLET11.WPP        831   01-01-80 01:09a
WPF1     .WPP     13,707   10-28-89 03:18p   WPF1-50 .WPP     13,706   10-28-89 03:04p
WPF1-AS .WPP      12,541   10-28-89 03:05p   WPF10    .WPP     10,849   10-29-89 10:02p
WPF10-50.WPP      10,849   10-29-89 10:02p   WPF10-AS.WPP      9,553   10-29-89 10:03p
WPF11    .WPP     14,922   01-01-80 07:09a   WPF11-50.WPP     14,922   01-01-80 07:09a
WPF11-AS.WPP      13,659   01-01-80 07:10a   WPF12    .WPP     11,767   01-01-80 01:45p
WPF12-50.WPP      11,767   01-01-80 01:45p   WPF12-AS.WPP     10,566   01-01-80 01:46p
WPF13    .WPP     13,206   01-01-80 04:13a   WPF13-50.WPP     13,206   01-01-80 04:13a
WPF13-AS.WPP      11,973   01-01-80 04:14a   WPF14    .WPP     13,816   11-07-89 09:52p
WPF14-50.WPP      13,809   11-07-89 09:53p   WPF14-AS.WPP     10,139   11-07-89 09:54p
WPF15    .WPP     10,445   11-10-89 04:39p   WPF15-50.WPP     10,445   11-10-89 04:41p
WPF15-AS.WPP       9,357   11-10-89 04:41p   WPF2     .WPP     17,127   10-29-89 09:12a
WPF2-50 .WPP      17,127   10-29-89 09:13a ▼ WPF2-AS .WPP     15,809   10-29-89 09:14a

1 Retrieve; 2 Delete; 3 Move/Rename; 4 Print; 5 Short/Long Display;
6 Look; 7 Other Directory; 8 Copy; 9 Find; N Name Search: 6
```

Figure 7-2. Screen with documents on the drive and directory

Q Retrieving a Document When You Don't Know the Name

1. Press F5 List Files or select List Files from the File menu.

   The current directory, path, and *.* for file name appears.

2. Enter a new drive and directory, if necessary, and press Enter.

   A screen appears showing the documents on the drive and directory you entered.

3. Highlight the document to be retrieved, and then select 1 Retrieve.

   The document is retrieved.

   ☐

From the List Files menu, you can move to another directory. For example, on the screen shown in Figure 7-3, the Parent directory is highlighted. "Parent" is another name for the superior or higher directory. Figure 7-4 shows the result after you press Enter with the Parent directory highlighted. The files of that directory appear. You can then select files from this screen.

79

```
01-01-80  12:35a            Directory C:\WP51\DOC\*.WPP
Document size:        0   Free: 14,325,760 Used:      665,278    Files:      63

.     Current   <Dir>             | ..    Parent    <Dir>
1-5      .WPP       884  01-01-80 12:11a | BELET    .WPP     984  10-22-89 09:46p
BELET10E.WPP     1,533  10-29-89 10:05p | BELET111.WPP   2,062  01-01-80 12:53a
BELET112.WPP     1,081  01-01-80 07:11a | BELET41 .WPP     519  10-22-89 09:00a
BELET42 .WPP       561  10-22-89 09:11a | BELET45 .WPP     568  10-22-89 01:20p
BELET53 .WPP       788  10-28-89 02:20p | BELET76 .WPP     967  10-22-89 09:33p
BELET04 .WPP       984  10-22-89 09:45p | BENLET11.WPP     831  01-01-80 01:09a
WPF1     .WPP    13,707  10-28-89 03:18p | WPF1-50 .WPP  13,706  10-28-89 03:04p
WPF1-AS .WPP    12,541  10-28-89 03:05p | WPF10   .WPP  10,849  10-29-89 10:02p
WPF10-50.WPP    10,849  10-29-89 10:02p | WPF10-AS.WPP   9,553  10-29-89 10:03p
WPF11    .WPP    14,922  01-01-80 07:09a | WPF11-50.WPP  14,922  01-01-80 07:09a
WPF11-AS.WPP    13,659  01-01-80 07:10a | WPF12   .WPP  11,767  01-01-80 01:45p
WPF12-50.WPP    11,767  01-01-80 01:45p | WPF12-AS.WPP  10,566  01-01-80 01:46p
WPF13    .WPP    13,206  01-01-80 04:13a | WPF13-50.WPP  13,206  01-01-80 04:13a
WPF13-AS.WPP    11,973  01-01-80 04:14a | WPF14   .WPP  13,816  11-07-89 09:52p
WPF14-50.WPP    13,809  11-07-89 09:53p | WPF14-AS.WPP  10,139  11-07-89 09:54p
WPF15    .WPP    10,445  11-10-89 04:39p | WPF15-50.WPP  10,445  11-10-89 04:41p
WPF15-AS.WPP     9,357  11-10-89 04:41p | WPF2    .WPP  17,127  10-29-89 09:12a
WPF2-50 .WPP    17,127  10-29-89 09:13a ▼ WPF2-AS .WPP  15,809  10-29-89 09:14a

1 Retrieve; 2 Delete; 3 Move/Rename; 4 Print; 5 Short/Long Display;
6 Look; 7 Other Directory; 8 Copy; 9 Find; N Name Search: 6
```

Figure 7-3. Parent directory highlighted

Caution: Do not press Enter after highlighting the document. If you do, the document will only be available for you to view; it will not be available for editing. Pressing Enter has the same effect as selecting 6 Look from the selections at the bottom of the screen.

```
01-01-80  12:37a              Directory C:\WP51\*.*
Document size:        0   Free: 14,321,664 Used:  3,928,590    Files:      104

  .    Current   <Dir>                  ..   Parent    <Dir>
 DOC      .       <Dir>   10-28-89 01:54p  LEARN    .     <Dir>   10-28-89 01:14p
 8514A   .URS    4,797   10-05-89 01:16p  ALTRNAT .WPK      919   10-11-89 11:32a
 ARROW-22.WPG      116   10-05-89 01:16p  ATI     .URS    4,937   10-05-89 01:16p
 BALLOONS.WPG    2,806   10-05-89 01:16p  BANNER-3.WPG      648   10-05-89 01:16p
 BICYCLE .WPG      607   10-05-89 01:16p  BKGRND-1.WPG   11,391   10-05-89 01:16p
 BORDER-8.WPG      144   10-05-89 01:16p  BULB    .WPG    2,030   10-05-89 01:16p
 BURST-1 .WPG      748   10-05-89 01:16p  BUTTRFLY.WPG    5,278   10-05-89 01:16p
 CALENDAR.WPG      300   10-05-89 01:16p  CERTIF  .WPG      608   10-05-89 01:16p
 CHARACTR.DOC   42,223   10-11-89 11:32a  CHARMAP .TST   40,696   10-05-89 01:16p
 CHKBOX-1.WPG      582   10-05-89 01:16p  CLOCK   .WPG    1,811   10-05-89 01:16p
 CNTRCT-2.WPG    2,678   10-05-89 01:16p  CODES   .WPM    5,117   10-11-89 11:32a
 CONVERT .EXE  105,201   10-11-89 11:32a  CURSOR  .COM    1,452   10-11-89 11:32a
 DEVICE-2.WPG      657   10-05-89 01:16p  DIPLOMA .WPG    2,342   10-05-89 01:16p
 EGA512  .FRS    3,584   10-05-89 01:16p  EGAITAL .FRS    3,584   10-05-89 01:16p
 EGASMC  .FRS    3,584   10-05-89 01:16p  EGAUND  .FRS    3,584   10-05-89 01:16p
 ENHANCED.WPK    3,355   10-11-89 11:32a  EQUATION.WPK    2,978   10-11-89 11:32a
 FIXBIOS .COM       50   10-11-89 11:32a  FLOPPY-2.WPG      404   10-05-89 01:16p
 GAVEL   .WPG      887   10-05-89 01:16p ▼ GENIUS  .URS   16,097   10-05-89 01:16p

1 Retrieve; 2 Delete; 3 Move/Rename; 4 Print; 5 Short/Long Display;
6 Look; 7 Other Directory; 8 Copy; 9 Find; N Name Search: 6
```

Figure 7-4. Parent directory files

Hint: If you are on the Document Selection screen and decide not to select a document, press F7 Exit to return to what you were doing before pressing F5 List Files.

Viewing, without Retrieving, a Document

If you have a lot of documents or a number of documents with similar names, viewing the Selection screen can be confusing. You may still have no clue as to the document to retrieve.

Retrieving the incorrect document and then repeating the process to find the correct one is time consuming and can be a little frustrating. WordPerfect gives you a way to avoid this situation by letting you look quickly at a document before retrieving it. You can easily look at several documents before retrieving the correct one.

To look at but not retrieve a document, start from a "blank" WordPerfect screen. Press F5 List Files or select List Files from the File menu. A message like the following appears:

```
Dir C: \WP51\DOC\*.*
```

This message displays the current drive; the path, if any; and *.* to indicate "all document names with all document extensions." Type in the drive and directory for which you want to list documents. Keep *.* in place of a document name. Press Enter. A screen appears showing the documents on your specified drive and directory. Highlight the name of the document you want to look at. Select 6 Look and the document will appear on your screen. Review the document, using the cursor arrow keys to *scroll* its text. This message at the bottom left of the screen reminds you how to return to your document listing:

81

```
Press EXIT when done
```

When you are done looking at the document, press F7 Exit. You are returned to the document list. Select another document or press F7 Exit to return to your document screen.

Q Look at without Retrieving a Document

1. Press F5 List Files or select List Files from the File menu.

   The current drive, path, and *.* for file name appear.

2. Type in drive, path, and file name information, if needed.

   A screen listing the documents appears.

3. Highlight the document name to retrieve and select 6 Look.

   The document is retrieved.

4. View the document and press F7 Exit when done.

You're returned to the document list.

5. Press F7 Exit to return to document screen.

The document screen appears.

Changing the Designated Drive and Directory

You can type in the drive and path every time you save a document, retrieve a document, or search for a document to retrieve. If you consistently use a drive and path different from the one that automatically appears, you may enter that drive and path to come up each time. The drive and path that Word-Perfect automatically brings up is the *default directory*. That is, if no other drive and directory path is indicated, the default directory is used.

To change the designated drive and directory, press F5 List Files or select List Files from the File menu. A message like the following appears:

```
Dir C: \WP51\*.*
```

This message displays the current drive; the path, if any; and *.* to indicate "all document names with all document extensions." Press Enter and a screen showing the documents on the drive and directory appears. Press 7 Other Directory. A message like this appears showing the current drive and directory:

```
New directory = C:\WP51
```

Type in the new drive and path information. Press Enter. A message like this appears, indicating the new drive, path, and files to select (*.* indicates all files):

```
Dir C:\WP51\DOC\*.*
```

Press F7 Exit. The files for that drive and directory appear. Press F7 Exit again and you are returned to your document.

82

The next time you list files, retrieve text, or save a document, this new default is used if no other drive or directory is designated.

You can cut short the process of setting a new designated drive. This approach bypasses several steps. Start by pressing F5 List Files or selecting List Files from the File menu. A message like the following appears:

```
Dir C: \WP51\*.*
```

This message displays the current drive; the path, if any; and *.* to indicate "all document names with all document extensions." Press an equal sign (=). A message like this one appears:

```
New directory = C:\WP51
```

83

Change the drive and directory as desired and press Enter. The new drive and directory appears like this:

```
Dir C: \WP51\DOC\*.*
```

Press Esc and you are returned to your document. The new drive and directory are set.

Ⓠ Shortcut to Change the Designated Drive and Directory

1. Press F5 List Files.	A message like the following appears: `Dir C: \WP51\*.*`
2. Press an equal sign (=).	A message like this one appears: `New directory = C:\WP51`
3. Change the drive and directory as desired and press Enter.	The new drive and directory appears like this: `Dir C: \WP51\DOC\*.*`
4. Press Esc.	The new drive and directory are set.

Retrieving One Document Into Another

If you have a document on the screen, then retrieve another document, the document you are retrieving is placed into the current document at your cursor position. This feature is useful for boilerplate text stored in a document that you want to retrieve into another document. It is also one way to copy the complete contents of one file into another file. (Chapter 19 covers other ways to copy from one document to another.)

Figure 7-5 shows our document prior to retrieving the boilerplate text "Sincerely, Barbara J. Wiley." The closing is held in a document called CLOSE.WPP and can be retrieved into any letter. Figure 7-6 illustrates the document with boilerplate retrieved into it.

84

```
File Edit Search Layout Mark Tools Font Graphics Help
───────────────────────────────────────────────────────

Mr. David Randolph
Bennington Corporation
45 Superstition Highway
Phoenix, Arizona 85252

Dear Mr. Randolph:

      As I discussed, I am very interested in pursuing a career with
the Bennington Corporation. My complete resume is attached.  I
look forward to speaking with you further on June 8th.  I'll meet
you at your corporate office location at 45 Superstition Highway.




                                         Doc 1 Pg 1 Ln 3" Pos 1"
```

Figure 7-5. Document before retrieving another document

Make sure the document you want to copy appears on your screen. Position your cursor in the location to be copied to. Use either of these two retrieval methods:

▶ Press Shift-F10 Retrieve Text or select Retrieve from the File menu, type in the document name, and press Enter. The document is retrieved.

```
File Edit Search Layout Mark Tools Font Graphics Help

Mr. David Randolph
Bennington Corporation
45 Superstition Highway
Phoenix, Arizona 85252

Dear Mr. Randolph:

     As I discussed, I am very interested in pursuing a career with
the Bennington Corporation. My complete resume is attached. I
look forward to speaking with you further on June 8th. I'll meet
you at your corporate office location at 45 Superstition Highway.

Sincerely,


Barbara J. Wiley




C:\WP51\DOC\BELET.WPP              Doc 1 Pg 1 Ln 3.67" Pos 1"
```

Figure 7-6. Document after retrieving another document

85

▶ Press F5 List Files or select List Files from the File
menu, enter the drive and path, then press Enter.
Highlight the document, select 1 Retrieve, and respond
y to this message:

Retrieve into current document? (Y/N) No

The document is retrieved.

Summary

In this chapter you've learned:

▶ If you know the name of the document to retrieve, use
Shift-F10 Retrieve Text.

▶ If you don't know the name of the document to retrieve,
use F5 List Text or select List Text from the File menu,
highlight the document to retrieve, and select
1 Retrieve.

▶ To look at the contents of a document (but not edit it),
use F5 List Text (or select List Text from the File

menu), highlight the document to view, and select
6 Look.

▶ To change the drive and directory designation, use F5
List Text (or select it from the File menu). Press the
equal sign and type in the new drive and directory or
proceed to select 7 Other Directory.

▶ To retrieve an entire document into another document,
place your cursor at the spot in the document to retrieve
to and use any retrieve method to move the second
document.

86

Chapter 8

Changing the Margins

In This Chapter

▶ *How to set the paper size and type*
▶ *How to set top and bottom margins*
▶ *How to set right and left margins*
▶ *What units of measure you may use*

Setting Margins

Margins are the amount of space from the edge of the paper to the text in your document. WordPerfect allows you to determine the size of your margins document by document. You can change margins within a document as often as you like.

Most WordPerfect users like to use inches to measure the margins. You may enter other units of measure, however, as described at the end of this chapter.

The procedure to control your margins is:

▶ Enter the paper size and type. This tells WordPerfect the dimensions of your paper.
▶ Identify the size of each margin: top, bottom, left, and right. WordPerfect will leave the margins as "white space."

▶ WordPerfect fits your text in the space that remains. As a result, the line length of the text you enter is determined by the measurement from the left to the right of the page minus the left and right margins. The number of lines that WordPerfect fits on a page is determined by the length of the page minus the top and bottom margins.

Figure 8-1 shows the edge of the paper, the margins, and the area left for WordPerfect to use for the letter.

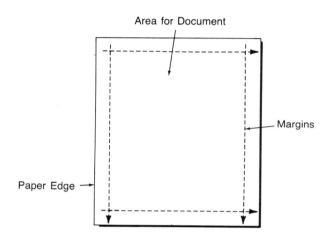

Figure 8-1. Paper edge, margins, and document area

When you set the paper size/type and margins, you will use the Format menu. As you can see in Figure 8-2, a variety of formatting options are included on this menu.

Setting the Paper Size and Type

The first step in controlling margins is to set the paper size and type. WordPerfect's default (the setting which comes already established in WordPerfect) is for 8 1/2 x 11″ paper of standard weight. This default handles most common stationery and computer or typing paper. Depending on how your printer works,

```
Format

    1 - Line
            Hyphenation              Line Spacing
            Justification            Margins Left/Right
            Line Height              Tab Set
            Line Numbering           Widow/Orphan Protection

    2 - Page
            Center Page (top to bottom)   Page Numbering
            Force Odd/Even Page           Paper Size/Type
            Headers and Footers           Suppress
            Margins Top/Bottom

    3 - Document
            Display Pitch            Redline Method
            Initial Codes/Font       Summary

    4 - Other
            Advance                  Overstrike
            Conditional End of Page  Printer Functions
            Decimal Characters       Underline Spaces/Tabs
            Language

Selection: 0
```

Figure 8-2. The Format menu

you may be able to use this setting for envelopes, too, and just
measure the address as if it were feeding like an 8 1/2 by 11"
sheet. For most work, you will not need to change the default
settings. In fact, you will only need to change the paper size or
type if you happen to use paper other than 8 1/2 x 11" size and a
different type, such as:

Bond
Letterhead
Labels
Envelopes
Transparencies
Cardstock
Other

If you want to change the default settings, place the cursor
in the location for entering the paper size/type code. Press
Shift-F8 Format, then press *2* page, or select Page on the Layout menu. Next, select 7 Paper Size/Type. The Format: Paper
Size menu appears. Enter the number for the size of paper you
are using. If your paper size is not included, type the letter *o*
(for Other), and enter the width, then height of the paper size.

You are next taken to the Format: Paper Type menu. Enter the number for the type of paper you are using. You are returned to the Format: Page menu. Complete another Format: Page option or press F7 Exit to return to your document. A code like this one is placed in your document and may be viewed using Reveal Codes:

[Paper Sz/Typ:8.5" x 11",Standard]

Setting Top and Bottom Margins

The top margin setting is the measurement from the top edge of your paper to where the first line of your document will print. The bottom margin is the measurement from the bottom edge of the paper to where you want the last line of the document printed. The top and bottom margins are 1" unless you change them.

Let's walk through setting the top and bottom margins on a letter. First, put the cursor at the top of the page. The code for the top and bottom margins will be inserted at this cursor location. Now, press Shift-F8 Format and *2* Page or select Page on the Layout menu. The Format: Page menu appears. Select 5 Margins Top and Bottom. The cursor goes to the Top field. To get a 2" top margin, type *2* and press Enter. The cursor goes to the Bottom field. To balance the letter, enter a 2" margin in the Bottom field and press Enter. The cursor returns to the Selection field at the bottom of the screen. Press F7 Exit to return to the letter. The top and bottom margins take effect. A code like this is inserted in the document:

[T/B Mar:2",2"]

 Setting the Top and Bottom Margins

1. Place the cursor where you want margin settings.	The code will be inserted at this spot.
2. Press Shift-F8 Format and *2* Page or select Page on the Layout menu.	The Format: Page menu appears.
3. Select 5 Margins Top and bottom.	Your cursor goes to the Top field.

4. Enter both measurements.

The cursor returns to the Selection field.

5. Press F7 Exit.

A code is inserted in your document and the margins take effect. □

Setting Right and Left Margins

The right margin is the space from the right edge of your paper to the rightmost characters of your document. The left margin is the space you want from the left edge of the paper to the left-most characters in the document. The left and right default margins are set to be 1″. You may change this setting.

Working with the letter again, place the cursor at the top of the page where the margin settings will take effect. Press Shift-F8 Format then *1* Line or select the Layout menu and then Line. The Format: Line menu appears. Select 7 Margins Left and Right. Your cursor goes to the Left field first. Enter 2 (for 2″) as the left margin and press Enter. You can just type the number 2 since inches is the default type of measurement. Your cursor then goes to the Right field. Enter 2″ as the right margin and press Enter. Your cursor goes back to the Selection field at the bottom of the screen. Press F7 Exit to go back to your document. After you do this, the code for the 2″ left and right margins appears in your document:

91

[L/R Mar:2″,2″]

Text produced after this code has been established will be affected by the new setting. Figure 8-3 shows our letter with 1-inch margins. Since 1-inch margins are WordPerfect's default, there is no code for the margins in the document. Figure 8-4 shows the letter after the margins have been changed to 2 inches. The lines in the letter are shortened and wrap around to accommodate the new, wider margins.

 Setting the Left and Right Margins

1. Position your cursor and press Shift-F8 Format then

The Format: Line menu appears.

```
Mr. David Randolph
Bennington Corporation
45 Superstition Highway
Phoenix, Arizona 85252

Dear Mr. Randolph:

        As I discussed, I am very interested in pursuing a career with
the Bennington Corporation.   My complete resume is attached.   I
look forward to speaking with you further on June 8th.   I'll meet
you at your corporate office location at 45 Superstition Highway.

Sincerely,


Barbara J. Wiley
```

Figure 8-3. BELET.WPP with 1-inch margins

```
              Mr. David Randolph
              Bennington Corporation
              45 Superstition Highway
              Phoenix, Arizona 85252

              Dear Mr. Randolph:

                      As I discussed, I am very interested in
              pursuing   a    career   with    the   Bennington
              Corporation.  My complete resume is attached.
              I look forward to speaking with you further on
              June 8th.    I'll meet you at your corporate
              office location at 45 Superstition Highway.

              Sincerely,


              Barbara J. Wiley
```

Figure 8-4. BELET.WPP with 2-inch margins

1 Line or select Line on the Layout menu.

2. Select 7 Margins Left and Right.

Your cursor goes to the Left field.

3. Enter the Left and Right margin measurements.

The cursor goes back to the Selection field.

4. Press F7 Exit to return to your document.

A code is inserted in the document. ☐

Setting the Unit of Measure

Most people who use WordPerfect keep "inches" as the default measurement for margins and other measures. Additionally, the status line identifies the location of your cursor in inches. For example, these status line values

Ln 2" Pos 5"

indicate that the line where your cursor rests is 2″ from the top edge of the paper and 5″ from the left edge of the paper.

I use inches and recommend you use it, too. Beside the familiarity, the beauty of using inches is that if you want to place characters on the page, you can pick up a ruler and simply measure margins or other format options.

You may have a special need for another unit of measure, though. The units of measure available in WordPerfect are shown in Table 8-1.

Table 8-1. WordPerfect's measurement unit options

Measurement	Notation
inches	i or ″
centimeters	c
points	p
1200ths of an inch	w
units for lines and columns	u

When you type in a type of measurement (such as a margin entry), you can enter the amount of the measurement followed by its notation. If inches is set as the default, the entry is converted to inches. For example, if you want a right margin to be 4 centimeters, enter 4c in the Right Margin field. If the default is inches, WordPerfect converts 4 centimeters to 1.57 inches and displays that amount. Points is a special measurement used with particular type styles. If you are using a laser printer you may want to use points occasionally.

WordPerfect allows you to control the measure used on menus along with the measure displayed in the status line. You can change the default for the unit of measurement.

To change the unit of measurement default, press Shift-F1 Setup or select Setup from the File menu. Select Environment. From the Setup: Environment screen, select *8* Units of Measure. The Setup: Units of Measure screen appears (see Figure 8-5). Press *1* Display and Entry of Numbers for Margins, Tabs, and so on. Enter the type of measurement (i or ", c, p, w, or u) to be shown in the Selection field. Press *2* Status Line Display. Enter the measure to be shown in the status line (i or ", c, p, w, or u). Press F7 Exit. The new defaults are set.

```
Setup: Units of Measure

    1 - Display and Entry of Numbers          "
          for Margins, Tabs, etc.

    2 - Status Line Display                   "


Legend:

    " = inches
    i = inches
    c = centimeters
    p = points
    w = 1200ths of an inch
    u = WordPerfect 4.2 Units (Lines/Columns)




Selection: 0
```

Figure 8-5. Setup: Units of Measure screen

Summary

In this chapter you've learned:

▶ You may enter the precise paper size and type you are using.

▶ Pressing Shift-F8 Format then 2 Page (or selecting Page on the Layout menu) is the route to set the Paper Size/Type and Top and Bottom Margin fields.

▶ Press Shift-F8 Format then 1 Line (or choose Line on the Layout menu) to lead in to setting Left and Right Margins.

▶ You have a variety of units of measures from which to choose. Inches is recommended as the default, however, unless you have a special circumstance.

95

Chapter 9

How to Print
Your Work

In This Chapter

▶ *How to set up your printer*
▶ *How to use Print*
▶ *How to print part of a document by blocking*
▶ *How to print a document on the disk (not on the screen)*
▶ *How to control the printing*

Setting Up Your Printer

When you installed WordPerfect, you identified the brand and type of the printer you are using. You must also perform some setup operations from within WordPerfect before you can use your printer.

Press Shift-F7 Print or select Print from the File menu. The Print menu (shown in Figure 9-1) appears.

Use the S - Select Printer option to select the printer feature. If you are using only one printer offering no fancy options, you probably only need to check that the name of the printer appears here.

```
Print

        1 - Full Document
        2 - Page
        3 - Document on Disk
        4 - Control Printer
        5 - Multiple Pages
        6 - View Document
        7 - Initialize Printer


Options

        S - Select Printer              HP LaserJet Series II (Basic)
        B - Binding Offset              0"
        N - Number of Copies            1
        U - Multiple Copies Generated by  WordPerfect
        G - Graphics Quality            Medium
        T - Text Quality                High




    Selection: 0
```

Figure 9-1. The Print menu

If you installed more than one printer and need to change the printer selected or need to set up options for fancy printing jobs (like working with a laser printer), press S - Select Printer. You are taken to the Printer: Select Printer screen, which shows you the printers that were installed. Actually, each line represents a file to run the printer indicated. You can select another printer with 1 Select. Or you might want to select 4 Copy in order to copy a file or 3 Edit in order to change the features of the selected printer.

Why copy or edit a printer file? You would only use this function if you were installing a printer with multiple options. For example, a laser printer might allow you to use several fonts (type styles). You might want to copy the file for the laser printer and then edit the new file to show a unique name and use a different set of fonts (type styles).

When you choose 3 Edit, the Select Printer: Edit menu (shown in Figure 9-2) appears. As you see in the Figure, you can edit the name, the *port* (connection to the computer), and features like the cartridges and fonts used with the printer file. Again, unless you have a pretty fancy printer, you will probably not need to change the information on this screen, but if you do, make any necessary edits now.

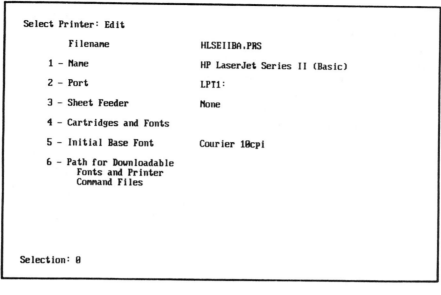

Figure 9-2. Select Printer: Edit menu

Press F7 Exit to return to the document screen when you have set up the printer.

Using Print

Once you have set up the printer, make sure your printer is ready to print:

▶ Is the cable between the printer and computer secure on both ends?

▶ Is the printer turned on? If not, make sure it is plugged in and then turn it on.

▶ Is the on-line light lit? If not, use the control panel to put the printer on-line (which means it is ready to receive your document from the computer).

▶ Is there paper in the printer and is it fed properly? If not, add paper and make sure it feeds smoothly into the printer.

Your printer should be ready, so with the document to print showing on your screen, press Shift-F7 Print or select Print from the File menu. The Print screen shown in Figure 9-1 appears.

To print more than one paper copy, select N - Number of Copies, type in the number of copies you want, and press Enter.

To print the entire document, select 1 - Full Document. To print only the page on which your cursor rests, select 2 - Page.

To "print" the document to a disk, select 3 - Document on Disk. When you print to a disk, you will be required to enter a name for the document before it is "printed." A DOS or ASCII file is created, which is not in WordPerfect format. This means the WordPerfect format symbols are removed, but the text itself remains intact.

100   Print a Document

1. With the document on the screen, press Shift-F7 Print or select Print from the File menu.	The Print menu appears.
2. Select N - Number of Copies and enter a number if you want more than one copy.	The number of copies appears.
3. Select 1 - Full Document to print the entire document, 2 - Page to print the page the cursor is on, or 3 - Document on Disk to print the document to a file (enter the name for the document).	The document prints.

Printing Only Part of a Document

If you want to print only part of a document, you may block the text to print and then press Shift-F7 Print or select Print from the File menu. This message appears:

Print block? No (Yes)

Type *y* and the block prints.

Printing a Document on the Disk

Sometimes you do not have to pull a document onto the screen to print it. Instead, you can print a document that resides on disk.

To print a document on disk, press F5 List Files or select List Files from the File menu. Make sure the drive and path for the files you want are entered at the prompt. For instance:

```
Dir C:\wp51\*.*
```

101

To have only document files appear, change the file designation from *.* to *.WPP (or whatever file extension you regularly use). Press Enter.

The List Files screen appears (shown in Figure 9-3). Use the cursor arrow keys to highlight the file you want to print. (In Figure 9-3 the BELET.WPP file is highlighted.)

```
01-01-80  12:47a             Directory C:\WP51\DOC\*.WPP
Document size:         0   Free: 14,307,328 Used:      665,278    Files:       63

.     Current    <Dir>                  ..    Parent    <Dir>
1-5      .WPP        804  01-01-80 12:11a   BELET    .WPP        984  10-22-89 09:46p
BELET10E.WPP      1,533  10-29-89 10:05p   BELET111.WPP      2,062  01-01-80 12:53a
BELET112.WPP      1,081  01-01-80 07:11a   BELET41  .WPP        519  10-22-89 09:00a
BELET42 .WPP        561  10-22-89 09:11a   BELET45  .WPP        568  10-22-89 01:20p
BELET53 .WPP        788  10-28-89 02:20p   BELET76  .WPP        967  10-22-89 09:33p
BELET84 .WPP        984  10-22-89 09:45p   BENLET11 .WPP        831  01-01-80 01:09a
WPF1     .WPP     13,707  10-28-89 03:18p   WPF1-50  .WPP     13,706  10-28-89 03:04p
WPF1-AS .WPP     12,541  10-28-89 03:05p   WPF10    .WPP     10,849  10-29-89 10:02p
WPF10-50.WPP     10,849  10-29-89 10:02p   WPF10-AS.WPP      9,553  10-29-89 10:03p
WPF11    .WPP     14,922  01-01-80 07:09a   WPF11-50 .WPP     14,922  01-01-80 07:09a
WPF11-AS.WPP     13,659  01-01-80 07:10a   WPF12    .WPP     11,767  01-01-80 01:45p
WPF12-50.WPP     11,767  01-01-80 01:45p   WPF12-AS.WPP     10,566  01-01-80 01:46p
WPF13    .WPP     13,206  01-01-80 04:13a   WPF13-50 .WPP     13,206  01-01-80 04:13a
WPF13-AS.WPP     11,973  01-01-80 04:14a   WPF14    .WPP     13,816  11-07-89 09:52p
WPF14-50.WPP     13,809  11-07-89 09:53p   WPF14-AS.WPP     10,139  11-07-89 09:54p
WPF15    .WPP     10,445  11-10-89 04:39p   WPF15-50 .WPP     10,445  11-10-89 04:41p
WPF15-AS.WPP      9,357  11-10-89 04:41p   WPF2     .WPP     17,127  10-29-89 09:12a
WPF2-50 .WPP     17,127  10-29-89 09:13a ▼ WPF2-AS  .WPP     15,809  10-29-89 09:14a

1 Retrieve; 2 Delete; 3 Move/Rename; 4 Print; 5 Short/Long Display;
6 Look; 7 Other Directory; 8 Copy; 9 Find; N Name Search: 6
```

Figure 9-3. The List Files screen

Select 4 Print and this prompt appears:

Page(s): All

Leave the number of pages "as is" to print the entire document or type in only those pages you want to print. Use a dash to indicate "through" or a comma to indicate "and." Here are some examples:

3-8   prints pages 3 through 8
3,8   prints pages 3 and 8

Once the pages to print are identified, press Enter. This message appears while the print order is sent to the printer:

* Please wait *

102

You are returned to the List Files screen. Press F7 Exit to return to your document. The pages you indicated will be printed.

Q **Printing from Disk**

1. Press Shift-F5 List Files or select List Files from the File menu.

The List Files screen appears.

2. Highlight the document to print and select 4 Print.

The prompt Page(s): All appears.

3. Type in the pages to print and press Enter.

The pages print.

4. Press F7 Exit to go back to your document.

You are returned to your document.

Controlling the Print

Sometimes after starting a print job, you change your mind. To control the print, press Shift-F7 Print, and then select 4 - Control Printer from the Print screen. The Print: Control Printer screen shown in Figure 9-4 appears. Notice that information about the "Current Job" (document being printed) appears. Then a "Job List" (the list of waiting documents) appears. Notice that each waiting job is assigned a number. Finally, the number of "Additional Jobs Not Shown" (if any) appears. The options from which you may select appear at the bottom of the screen.

```
Print: Control Printer

Current Job

Job Number: 6                              Page Number:  None
Status:      Starting print job           Current Copy: None
Message:     None
Paper:       None
Location:    None
Action:      None


Job List

Job   Document              Destination      Print Options
 6    (Screen)              LPT 1



Additional Jobs Not Shown: 0



1 Cancel Job(s); 2 Rush Job; 3 Display Jobs; 4 Go (start printer); 5 Stop: 0
```

103

Figure 9-4. Print: Control Printer screen

To control a print job, select one of these options:

1 - Cancel Job(s): to cancel the print. Enter the number of the job (shown in the Job List on this screen) and press Enter. To cancel all jobs, type in an asterisk (*) and press Enter.

2 - Rush Job: to move a print job ahead of other documents waiting to be printed. Identify the number of the job to be printed next and press Enter.

3 - Display Jobs: to see which jobs are waiting to print if "Additional Jobs Not Shown" has a value. If all jobs are displayed on the screen when you make this selection, WordPerfect lets you know with a message.

4 - Go (start printer): to start the printer after it has been stopped.

5 - *Stop*: to stop the printer to adjust paper or perform another activity. Use 4 - Go to start the printer again.

Summary

In this chapter you've learned:

▶ Select your printer by pressing Shift-F7 Print or by selecting Print from the File menu. The S - Select Printer option on the Printer screen is the avenue to select the printer or edit printer functions.

▶ To print a document or a page, or to print a document to a file, press Shift-F7 Print or select Print from the File menu. The option you select handles the document on the screen.

▶ You may block the text to print and then press Shift-F7 Print or select Print from the File menu.

▶ To print a document from a disk, press F5 List Files or select List Files from the File menu. Highlight the file and select 4 Print.

▶ To control a print, press Shift-F7 Print or select Print from the File menu. Select 4 - Control Printer on the Print menu and make your control selection.

Chapter 10
Placing Text on a Line

In This Chapter

► *Indenting text: why and how*
► *How to center text*
► *How to place text flush right on the page*
► *How to justify text*
► *How to control line spacing*
► *How to create initial codes*

Indenting Text

Indenting text aligns the text according to margins. Using indent options is different from using the Tab key. When you use the Tab key, only the first line is indented. When you use WordPerfect's indent feature, you indent as many lines as you wish until you press the Enter key to end a paragraph.

For example, text with indents has been added to the letter shown in Figure 10-1. Each paragraph starts with a Tab, so only the paragraph's first line is indented. The list of attachments is an example of the use of WordPerfect's left indent feature. Each dash is followed by an indent, followed by text. Notice that the first line of attachments wraps around to line up with the indented text above. Later in the letter, a quote is indented from both the right and left.

```
File Edit Search Layout Mark Tools Font Graphics Help
───────────────────────────────────────────────────────
   Dear Mr. Randolph:

       As I discussed, I am very interested in
   pursuing a career with the Bennington
   Corporation.  I have attached:

   -    My resume with a chronological work histo-
        ry as requested
   -    Letters of recommendation
   -    Certificates of achievement

       Your friend, Jim Miller, recently ap-
   plauded my work on our exposition with these
   remarks at the dinner presentation:

       "Barbara has consistently proven
       that she goes above and beyond our
       expectations.  And... always within
       budget no less!"

       I look forward to speaking with you
   further on June 8th.  I'll meet you at your
                        Doc 1 Pg 1 Ln 6.67" Pos 2"
```

Figure 10-1. Text with indents

As illustrated, you may indent from the left or from both the right and left with WordPerfect. A third type of indent is a *hanging indent*, which leaves the first line of the paragraph at the left margin and indents the following lines at the next tab stop.

All indents align with the tab settings in WordPerfect. For now, you should work with the default tab settings. (Chapter 11 covers how to change tab settings.)

Setting Left Indent

To indent text on the left only, press F4 Left Indent until the appropriate tab stop is reached. An Indent code is embedded in your text. Type in the text you want indented; it automatically aligns with the last indent entered. When you press Enter, the indent is completed.

Setting Left and Right Indent

To indent text on the left and right, press Shift-F4 for Left/Right Indent. The code is placed in your text. Type in the text. The text aligns along the left tab stop and an equal distance from the right side. When you press Enter, the indent is completed.

Setting Hanging Indent

To leave the first line of a paragraph at the margin and indent the rest of the paragraph, press F4 Left Indent then Shift-Tab Margin Release. Both the Indent and Margin Release codes are placed in the document. When you type in the text and press Enter, the first line remains at the left margin and subsequent lines are indented.

107

Indenting Existing Text

You may apply all the indent options to existing text. Just insert the indent code(s) where you want the indents created.

Centering Text

The old-fashioned way of centering text was to count the number of characters in the text to be entered, subtract that number from the number of characters possible in the line, divide by two, space in that number of spaces, and begin typing. This tedious operation is replaced with the Shift-F6 Center key combination.

Just place your cursor in the line and press Shift-F6 Center. A code is placed in your text and the cursor goes to the center of the line. Type in your text. As you type, the characters move to the left or right to even the centering. When you are done, press Enter.

Figure 10-2 illustrates centered text with Barbara J. Wiley's return address.

```
File Edit Search Layout Mark Tools Font Graphics Help
─────────────────────────────────────────────────────────

         Dear Mr. Randolph:

             As I discussed, I am very interested in
         pursuing a career with the Bennington
         Corporation.  I have attached:

         -    My resume with a chronological work histo-
              ry as requested
         -    Letters of recommendation
         -    Certificates of achievement

             Your friend, Jim Miller, recently ap-
         plauded my work on our exposition with these
         remarks at the dinner presentation:

             "Barbara has consistently proven
             that she goes above and beyond our
             expectations.  And... always within
             budget no less!"

             I look forward to speaking with you
         further on June 8th.  I'll meet you at your
C:\WP51\DOC\BELET112.WPP                    Doc 1 Pg 1 Ln 6.67" Pos 3.4"
```

Figure 10-2. Centered text

You may center existing text. Just block the text and press Shift-F6 Center. This message appears:

`[Just:Center]? No (Yes)`

Select Yes to center the text. The text in the block is centered and the appropriate code(s) inserted.

Placing Text Flush Right

Figure 10-3 demonstrates the flush-right option on the date line. You don't have to count text or backspaces; just press Alt-F6 Flush Right. Your cursor goes to the right margin. As you type in the text, it moves left. Press Enter and the text aligns with the right margin.

To make existing text flush right, place the cursor before the text and press Alt-F6 Flush Right.

```
File Edit Search Layout Mark Tools Font Graphics Help
                      Barbara J. Wiley
                      3421 Pecos Way
                 San Diego, California 92123

       Mr. David Randolph
       Bennington Corporation
       45 Superstition Highway
       Phoenix, Arizona 85252

                            May 12, 1991

       Dear Mr. Randolph:

             As I discussed, I am very interested in
       pursuing a career with the Bennington
       Corporation.  I have attached:

       -     My resume with a chronological work histo-
             ry as requested
       -     Letters of recommendation
C:\WP51\DOC\BELET112.WPP                   Doc 1 Pg 1 Ln 1" Pos 3.45"
```

Figure 10-3. Flush right date

109

Justifying Text

Justification refers to the even vertical alignment of text in a document. When you enter a justification code all the text that follows that code will be justified. WordPerfect's default is called *full justification*, which lines up text evenly between right and left margins. Figure 10-4 shows our letter with full justification.

WordPerfect makes four types of justification possible:

▶ Left justification for most documents
▶ Right justification for special layouts
▶ Full justification (text aligned evenly on left and right margins) for a formal appearance
▶ Center justification (text centered on every line) for special layouts

Figure 10-5 illustrates an advertising piece with each type of justification applied.

```
                    Barbara J. Wiley
                     3421 Pecos Way
               San Diego, California 92123


        Mr. David Randolph
        Bennington Corporation
        45 Superstition Highway
        Phoenix, Arizona 85252

                                      May 12, 1991

        Dear Mr. Randolph:

            As I discussed, I am very interested in
        pursuing   a   career   with   the   Bennington
        Corporation.  I have attached:

        -    My resume with a chronological work histo-
             ry as requested
        -    Letters of recommendation
        -    Certificates of achievement

            Your friend, Jim Miller, recently ap-
        plauded my work on our exposition with these
        remarks at the dinner presentation:

             "Barbara  has  consistently  proven
             that she goes above and beyond our
             expectations.  And... always within
             budget no less!"

            I  look  forward  to  speaking  with  you
        further on June 8th.  I'll meet you at your
        corporate office location at 45 Superstition
        Highway.


        Sincerely,


        Barbara J. Wiley
```

Figure 10-4. Letter with full justification

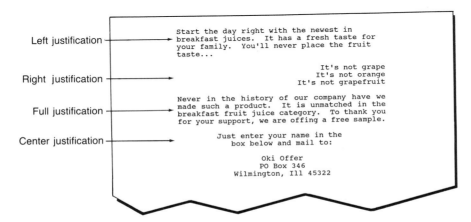

Figure 10-5. Four types of justification

To justify text, place the cursor where you want to begin the justification. Press Shift-F8 Format and then select *1* Line or choose Line from the Layout menu. The Format: Line menu appears. Select 3 - Justification. A line like this appears:

Justification: 1 Left; 2 Center; 3 Right; 4 Full:

Select the type of justification you want. A justification code is placed in your document at the cursor location. The text that follows this code is justified accordingly. To remove or change the justification, delete the first code or enter the code for another type of justification.

Controlling Line Spacing

Line spacing refers to the number of lines between each printed line. The default is single spacing. However, you can double space or triple space or space by any number of lines you want to enter. Just press Shift-F8 Format and select 1 Line or choose Line from the Layout menu. Select 6 - Line Spacing and enter the number of lines (*1* for single space, *2* for double space, and so on). Press Enter. Press F7 Exit when you want to return to your document. A code like this is placed in the document:

[Ln Spacing: 3]

The text entered after the code reflects the line spacing you set.

 **Line Spacing**

1. Press Shift-F8 Format and type *1* Line or select Line from the Layout menu.

   The Format: Line menu appears.

2. Select 6 - Line Spacing, enter the number of lines, and press Enter. Press F7 Exit to return to your document.

   The text following the inserted code follows the new line spacing setting.

Initial Codes

You may want to change some of WordPerfect's defaults. For example, you may want to change WordPerfect's default of single-line spacing. If you typically use double spacing, you may get tired of having to set the line spacing for each document. You can change this initial code (and others) through the Initial Code option.

To change a default, press Shift-F1 Setup and select 4 - Initial Settings on the Setup menu. Or you can start with the File menu and select Setup, then Initial Settings. From the Setup: Initial Settings menu, select 5 - Initial Codes. You are taken to the Initial Codes screen like that shown in Figure 10-6. Enter the new line spacing or any other codes you want as the new default(s). Save the entries by pressing F7 Exit until you return to your document. These initial codes are applied to every document you create from then on until you change the codes again.

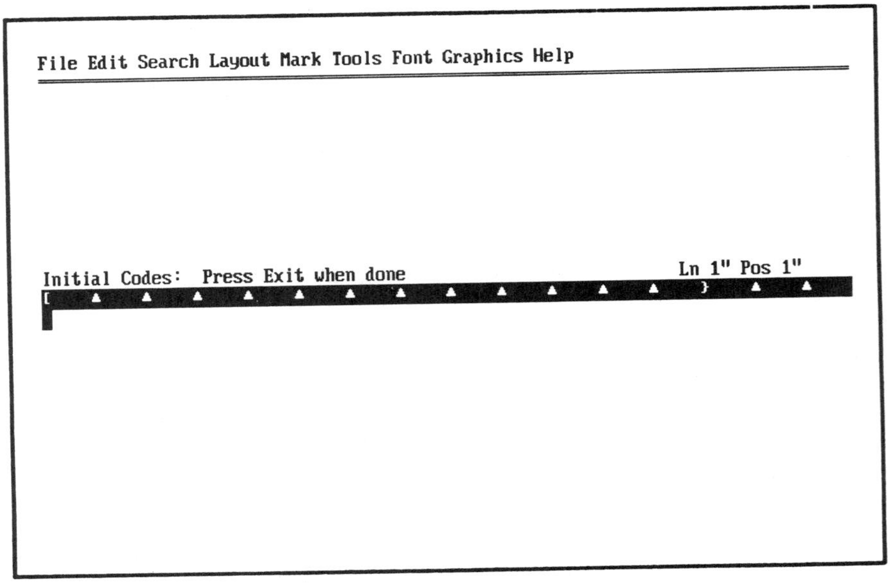

File Edit Search Layout Mark Tools Font Graphics Help

Initial Codes: Press Exit when done   Ln 1" Pos 1"

Figure 10-6. Initial Codes screen

⊘ **Caution:** The initial codes become new defaults. The codes for the settings don't appear in your document. Therefore, if you give your document on a disk to someone with different initial codes, your settings will not be in place.

Summary

In this chapter you've learned:

- ▶ You may enter three types of indented text: F4 Left Indent, Shift-F4 Right and Left Indent, and F4 Left Indent followed by Ctrl-Tab Margin Release (for a hanging indent).
- ▶ Use Shift-F6 Center to center text.
- ▶ Use Alt-F6 Flush Right to place text even with the right margin.
- ▶ You may use the Line option of the Layout menu to select from four types of justification: left, right, full, or centered.
- ▶ Use the Layout menu, Line option, to control line spacing.
- ▶ You may change the default initial codes from the File menu, by choosing Setup and then the Initial Settings option.

113

Chapter 11
Using Tabs

In This Chapter

▶ *The types of tabs available*
▶ *How to add or delete tabs*
▶ *How to add dot leaders*
▶ *How to add headings*
▶ *How to change decimal/align characters*
▶ *How to use Tab Align*

Default Tabs

A tab in WordPerfect is like a tab setting on a typewriter, only better. At the basic level, you press the Tab key or Indent, your cursor moves to the next column marked by a tab setting, and a tab or insert code appears in your text. At a more sophisticated level, according to the type of tab stop you enter, you can align characters on the left, on the right, by any character, or you can center the characters.

WordPerfect comes with defaults of tab settings every half inch. The resume entry shown in Figure 11-1 was created with WordPerfect default tab settings. Notice that with tabs set every half inch, the Indent key had to be pressed several times to complete the entries. As you'll learn later in this chapter, you can set new tab settings anywhere you like. By entering your own tab settings, you can reduce the number of times you have to press the Tab or Indent key.

```
File Edit Search Layout Mark Tools Font Graphics Help
─────────────────────────────────────────────────────────────

Experience:

    1988-present    Programmer    Barney Corporation, 4566
                                  Oakway, Austin, Texas 78759
                                  (512) 253-9900.

                                  Cobol and PL1 in an IBM
                                  environment.
C:\WP51\DOC\BENLET.WPP                           Doc 1 Pg 2 Ln 3" Pos 4.5"
[    ▲    ▲    ▲    ▲    ▲    ▲    ▲    ▲    ▲    ▲    ▲    }   ▲    ▲
(512) 253[-]9900.[HRt]
[HRt]
[→Indent][→Indent][→Indent][→Indent][→Indent][→Indent][→Indent]Cobol and PL1 in
an IBM[SRt]
environment.[HRt]
[HRt]
[HRt]
[HRt]
Education:[HRt]
[HRt]

Press Reveal Codes to restore screen
```

Figure 11-1. Resume with default tabs

Types of Tabs

WordPerfect allows you to choose from four types of tabs:

► Left
► Decimal
► Center
► Right

The fund-raising activities included on the resume shown in Figure 11-2 illustrate each type of tab stop. A description of each type follows.

```
File Edit Search Layout Mark Tools Font Graphics Help


Barbara J. Wiley's Work Related Fundraising Activities

    United Way Chair   10,500.00    Children's Home      Feb 1990
    Committee Chair     1,200.00    Lunch Garden        June 1989
    Committee Chair       560.00    Flags for Flag Day    Ap 1989



C:\WP51\DOC\BELET.WPP                      Doc 1 Pg 1 Ln 1" Pos 1"
[      ▲              ▲              ▲             }        ▲
[Tab Set:Rel: -1",-0.5",+0.5",+2.9",+4.5",+6.5",+7.5",+8",+8.5",+9",+9.5",+10",+
10.5",+11",+11.5",+12",+12.5",+13"][HRt]
Barbara J. Wiley's Work Related Fundraising Activities[HRt]
[HRt]
[Tab]United Way Chair[Dec Tab]10,500.00[Cntr Tab]Children's Home[Rgt Tab]Feb 199
0[HRt]
[Tab]Committee Chair[Dec Tab]1,200.00[Cntr Tab]Lunch Garden[Rgt Tab]June 1989[HR
t]
[Tab]Committee Chair[Dec Tab]560.00[Cntr Tab]Flags for Flag Day[Rgt Tab]Ap 1989


Press Reveal Codes to restore screen
```

Figure 11-2. Types of tab stops

Left Tab Stop

The left tab stop is the default used by WordPerfect. When you use a left tab stop and then begin typing, the text is entered one space to the right of the tab stop. The [Tab] code is placed in your text. In Figure 11-2, the titles (such as Chairperson) are aligned under the standard left tab stop.

Decimal Tab Stop

You set a decimal tab stop to align text under the decimal tab setting. Text you type in is entered to the left of the decimal tab until you press the decimal point (a period). The [Dec Tab] code is entered into the text. Then the text is entered to the right. This feature is especially helpful when you want to enter columns of financial figures, as in Figure 11-2, where the money raised is aligned under the decimal point.

Center Tab Stop

The center tab is used to center text under the tab stop. As you type, the text is centered automatically, just like when you use the Shift-F6 Center function. Setting a center tab stop enables you to enter text before and after the centered text, as is shown in Figure 11-2. You can also see that the [Cntr Tab] code is entered into the text.

Right Tab Stop

The right tab is used to align text on the right character. As you enter text, it moves left until you finish typing. The code [Rgt Tab] appears in the text. In Figure 11-2 the year is entered using the right tab stop, which makes for an even right margin. You can, however, place the right tab stop anywhere in a line.

To use each of these tab stops, you don't need to press special keys, only the standard Tab or Indent keys. You do, however, need to set tab stops to tell WordPerfect where to place the tabs and what type of tab stop to use.

Changing Tab Stops

You may change tab stops to use any of the four types of tab options. First, identify where you want tab stops placed. For example, you may know where on the page you want tab settings. This is usually true if you want to print on a preprinted form and want characters to align precisely. To determine an exact location, just measure your page and identify the location of the tab stops from the left edge of the page. Or, you can "eyeball" the tab locations and begin entering new tab stops. You will have to visualize the tab stop effect as you work.

To add or delete tab stops, use the Shift-F8 Format key and then select 1 Line. Or you can select Line from the Layout pull-down menu. On the Format: Line menu, you'll see the 8 Tab Set option. The current tab setting is indicated. "Abs" means "Absolute," which is WordPerfect's convoluted way of saying that the tab settings are measured from the edge of the paper and not from your left margin. So, setting a tab stop at 3″ means the tab stop will be 3″ from the left edge of the paper not 3″ from the left margin setting.

Select 8 Tab Set. You are taken to the tab line shown in Figure 11-3. As you can see in this figure, the left tab stop is identified by an L, the decimal tab stop is identified by a D, a center tab stop is shown as a C, and the right tab stop appears as an R. Notice that the line is like a ruler, marking off the inches.

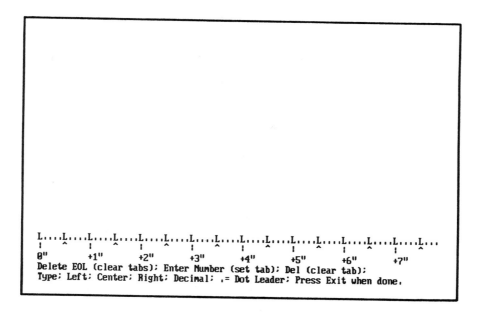

Figure 11-3. Tab line

You can add a tab setting simply by typing in a L, D, C, or R in the position desired. Once the tabs are entered, press F7 Exit until you return to your document. A code like that shown in Figure 11-4 appears to tell you that tabs other than the defaults have been entered. Delete a tab by pressing Delete or Backspace. To delete all the tab settings at once, press Home, Home, and Left Arrow. Then press Ctrl-End Delete End of Line. (This is faster than deleting a lot of tabs individually.)

```
File Edit Search Layout Mark Tools Font Graphics Help
──────────────────────────────────────────────────────────

Barbara J. Wiley's Work Related Fundraising Activities

    United Way Chair  10,500.00    Children's Home    Feb 1990
    Committee Chair    1,200.00    Lunch Garden      June 1989
    Committee Chair      560.00    Flags for Flag Day  Ap 1989




                                    Doc 1 Pg 1 Ln 1" Pos 1"
████████████████████████████████████████████████████████████
[Tab Set:Rel: -1",-0.5",+0.5",+2.9",+4.5",+6.5",+7.5",+8",+8.5",+9",+9.5",+10",+
10.5",+11",+11.5",+12",+12.5",+13"][HRt]
Barbara J. Wiley's Work Related Fundraising Activities[HRt]
[HRt]
[Tab]United Way Chair[Dec Tab]10,500.00[Cntr Tab]Children's Home[Rgt Tab]Feb 199
0[HRt]
[Tab]Committee Chair[Dec Tab]1,200.00[Cntr Tab]Lunch Garden[Rgt Tab]June 1989[HR
t]
[Tab]Committee Chair[Dec Tab]560.00[Cntr Tab]Flags for Flag Day[Rgt Tab]Ap 1989

Press Reveal Codes to restore screen
```

Figure 11-4. Code signifying tabs set

120

Q Adding and Deleting Tabs

1. Place your cursor where you want the new tab settings.

   Text after the location will be affected.

2. Press Shift-F8 Format and type *1* Line or select Line from the Layout menu.

   The Format: Line menu appears.

3. Select 8 Tab Set.

   The tab line appears.

4. Position your cursor and use the delete key or backspace key to delete tab settings. Or, type in an *L*, *D*, *C*, or *R* to add a tab setting.

   The tab settings appear on the tab line.

5. Press F7 Exit until you return to your document and begin using the tab settings.

   A tab stop code is entered in your document and text you enter after the code is affected. □

There are three benefits to becoming familiar with how to set tab stops. First, you can use all four types of tabs instead of being stuck with left tabs only. Second, by setting your own tab stops, you can reduce the number of times you have to press Tab or Indent. Third, you can use tabs to easily change the layout of your text. Simply by entering a new set of tab stops, the text after those tab stops is rearranged.

When resetting tabs, as long as you keep your first tab-setting code and, following it, enter the new tab-setting code you want, you can always change your mind and go back to your original setting. Just highlight the second tab-setting code on the Reveal Code screen and press Delete. The second set of codes is deleted and the text is reformatted to its original position.

In Figure 11-5 you see an example of changing tab settings and then reverting to the old ones. A new set of codes has been entered in the figure, moving the text. Notice that the original code is still in the text and the new tab-setting code follows. The resulting look of the document is a little crowded. To go back to the old tab settings, the second tab-setting code is deleted, and the text is restored to its earlier appearance.

121

```
File Edit Search Layout Mark Tools Font Graphics Help

Barbara J. Wiley's Work Related Fundraising Activities

        United Way Chair10,500.00  Children's Home Feb 1990
        Committee Chair  1,200.00    Lunch Garden  June 1989
        Committee Chair     560.00Flags for Flag Day Ap 1989



                                      Doc 1 Pg 1 Ln 1" Pos 1"
[     ▲              ▲          ▲              }         ▲
[Tab Set:Rel: -1",-0.5",+0.5",+2.9",+4.5",+6.5",+7.5",+8",+8.5",+9",+9.5",+10",+
10.5",+11",+11.5",+12",+12.5",+13"][Tab Set:Rel: -1",-0.5",+0.7",+2.9",+4.1",+5.
8",+7.5",+8",+8.5",+9",+9.5",+10",+10.5",+11",+11.5",+12",+12.5",+13"][HRt]
Barbara J. Wiley's Work Related Fundraising Activities[HRt]
[HRt]
[Tab]United Way Chair[Dec Tab]10,500.00[Cntr Tab]Children's Home[Rgt Tab]Feb 199
0[HRt]
[Tab]Committee Chair[Dec Tab]1,200.00[Cntr Tab]Lunch Garden[Rgt Tab]June 1989[HR
t]
[Tab]Committee Chair[Dec Tab]560.00[Cntr Tab]Flags for Flag Day[Rgt Tab]Ap 1989

Press Reveal Codes to restore screen
```

Figure 11-5. New tab code

> ► **Hint:** Once you are in the Tab line after selecting 8 Tab, you will enter a tab stop code whether you press F7 Exit or Escape to leave the line. To stop the operation and *not* enter the new tab settings, press F1 Cancel.

Dot Leaders

122

Occasionally, you may want to enter a row of dots (called *dot leaders*) between the text at tab settings. In Figure 11-6, dot leaders have been added to some of the tab settings. In effect, dots are entered when you move to the tab setting with a tab or indent.

```
Barbara J. Wiley's Work Related Fundraising Activities

     United Way Chair. 10,500.00 . . .Children's Home. . Feb 1990
     Committee Chair . .1,200.00 . . . Lunch Garden. . .June 1989
     Committee Chair . . .560.00 . .Flags for Flag Day . .Ap 1989












 . . . . .L . . . . . . . . . . . . . . . . . . . . . . .D . . . . . . . . . . . . . . . .C . . . . . . . . . . . . . . . . . . . .R . . . . . . . . .L . . .
 :      ^      :      ^      :      ^      :      ^      :      ^      :      ^      :      ^      :
 0"        +1"        +2"        +3"        +4"        +5"        +6"        +7"
 Delete EOL (clear tabs); Enter Number (set tab); Del (clear tab);
 Type; Left; Center; Right; Decimal; .= Dot Leader; Press Exit when done.
```

Figure 11-6. Dot leaders added to the text

To enter a tab stop to include dot leaders, place the cursor on a left (L), right (R), or decimal (D) tab in the tab line and type a period. The tab setting is in reverse video (light letter on a dark box or vice versa). When you use the tab stop, dot leaders appear.

Note that you cannot enter dot leaders before a center tab stop.

Entering Headings

Often, when you use tab stops, you are creating columns of text for which you want headings. You can use the tab stops, place your headings before the code to use earlier tab stops, or just type in the headings without using tab stops.

For example, in the sample resume, headings entered using the existing tab stops are shown in Figure 11-7. These headings are not as pleasing as those shown in Figure 11-8, which are entered without using the Tab or Indent key.

123

⊘ **Caution:** Some printers do not measure the spaces between tab stops and the spaces entered with the spacebar in the same way. Thus, your headings can appear lined up on the screen but not when printed. You may need to experiment with your printer to get the outcome desired.

Changing the Decimal/Align Character

The default decimal/align character is a period. When you use decimal tab stops, you type in a period as the alignment character and the text lines up according to the period. You can use any character, however, not just a period, to align by. For example, you might want to align text on an equal sign as shown here:

$$6 + 9 + 4 = 19$$
$$8 + 2 = 10$$
$$800 + 310 = 1110$$

```
File Edit Search Layout Mark Tools Font Graphics Help

Barbara J. Wiley's Work Related Fundraising Activities

    Position. . . . $ Raised. . . . . . .Purpose. . . . . . Date

    United Way Chair. 10,500.00 . . .Children's Home. . Feb 1990
    Committee Chair . .1,200.00 . . . Lunch Garden. . .June 1989
    Committee Chair . . .560.00 . .Flags for Flag Day . .Ap 1989

                                         Doc 1 Pg 1 Ln 1.5" Pos 7.5"
[      ▲             ▲             ▲            }      ▲
[Tab Set:Rel: -1",-0.5",+0.5",+2.9",+4.5",+6.5",+7.5",+8",+8.5",+9",+9.5",+10",+
10.5",+11",+11.5",+12",+12.5",+13"][Tab Set:Rel: -1",-0.5",+0.5",+2.9",+4.5",+6.
5",+7.5",+8",+8.5",+9",+9.5",+10",+10.5",+11",+11.5",+12",+12.5",+13"][HRt]
Barbara J. Wiley's Work Related Fundraising Activities[HRt]
[HRt]
[Tab]Position[Dec Tab]$ Raised[Cntr Tab]Purpose[Rgt Tab]Date[HRt]
[HRt]
[Tab]United Way Chair[Dec Tab]10,500.00[Cntr Tab]Children's Home[Rgt Tab]Feb 199
0[HRt]
[Tab]Committee Chair[Dec Tab]1,200.00[Cntr Tab]Lunch Garden[Rgt Tab]June 1989[HR

Press Reveal Codes to restore screen
```

Figure 11-7. Headings entered using existing tab stops

```
File Edit Search Layout Mark Tools Font Graphics Help

Barbara J. Wiley's Work Related Fundraising Activities

    Position          $ Raised        Purpose         Date

    United Way Chair. 10,500.00 . . .Children's Home. . Feb 1990
    Committee Chair . .1,200.00 . . . Lunch Garden. . .June 1989
    Committee Chair . . .560.00 . .Flags for Flag Day . .Ap 1989

                                         Doc 1 Pg 1 Ln 1.5" Pos 6.6"
[      ▲             ▲             ▲            }      ▲
[Tab Set:Rel: -1",-0.5",+0.5",+2.9",+4.5",+6.5",+7.5",+8",+8.5",+9",+9.5",+10",+
10.5",+11",+11.5",+12",+12.5",+13"][Tab Set:Rel: -1",-0.5",+0.5",+2.9",+4.5",+6.
5",+7.5",+8",+8.5",+9",+9.5",+10",+10.5",+11",+11.5",+12",+12.5",+13"][HRt]
Barbara J. Wiley's Work Related Fundraising Activities[HRt]
[HRt]
[Tab]Position          $ Raised        Purpose      ▌ Date[HRt]
[HRt]
[Tab]United Way Chair[Dec Tab]10,500.00[Cntr Tab]Children's Home[Rgt Tab]Feb 199
0[HRt]
[Tab]Committee Chair[Dec Tab]1,200.00[Cntr Tab]Lunch Garden[Rgt Tab]June 1989[HR

Press Reveal Codes to restore screen
```

Figure 11-8. Headings entered without using existing tab stops

To change the decimal/align character, press Shift-F8 Format then select 4 Other or select Other from the Layout menu. You are taken to the Format: Other menu. Select 3 Decimal/Align Character. Type in the keyboard character you want to use for the alignment and press Enter. Press F7 Exit to go back to your document. A code like this appears in your document identifying the decimal/align character:

`[Decml/Algn Char:=,,]`

The character after *Char:* is the new decimal/align character that will be used in text entered after the code. In this example, it is the equal sign. You may return to the period as the decimal/align character any time by deleting the code or by setting a period as the new decimal/align character.

125

Tab Align

Sometimes, you might want to align characters by the decimal/align character without changing to a decimal tab stop. For example, if you want to enter only a few lines of text aligned by a decimal/align character, it would be cumbersome to change the tab stop to a decimal tab stop, enter the text, then change the tab stop back to a left tab stop for the remainder of the document. Instead, you can use a key combination to use a tab stop temporarily as a decimal tab stop.

Place your cursor before the tab stop under which you want to align the character. Press Ctrl-F6 Align Character. The [DEC TAB] code appears in your document and the cursor goes under the next tab stop. This message appears at the bottom left of your screen to remind you which character is set as the current decimal/align character:

`Align char = =`

(In this case, the equal sign (=) is the decimal/align character.) Now as you type in text, it moves to the left. When you press the decimal/align character, the next text you type in will move to the right of the equal sign.

The Ctrl-F6 Tab Align feature affects your work with a single tab stop in a single line. You can use the feature again and again. Use Tab Align (instead of setting a decimal tab stop) when you only want to enter a few decimal tabs.

Summary

In this chapter you've learned:

▶ You use Shift-F8 Format then select 1 Line (or select Line from the Layout menu) to kick off entering left, decimal, center, or right tabs.

▶ From the tab line, you may enter an L, D, C, or R to enter new tabs or use Delete to delete tabs.

▶ To add dot leaders, type a period over the tab stop letter on the tab line.

▶ You may type in a heading with or without the tabs.

▶ To set a new decimal/align character, select Shift-F8 Format and 4 Other or select Other from the Layout menu. Continue by following the prompts.

▶ To temporarily align text by the decimal/align character, use Ctrl-F6 Tab Align.

126

Creating Multiple-Page Documents

In This Chapter

▶ *How WordPerfect automatically breaks pages*
▶ *How to create a new page yourself*
▶ *How to move between pages*
▶ *How to keep text from being split between pages*

Creating Multiple Pages

Okay, so you can create and print a document now. . .complete with the tab settings of your choice. You're ready to create a document that is more than one page long.

WordPerfect allows you to create lengthy documents. In fact, the only limit to the number of pages in a document depends on how much you can store and easily manipulate. Personally, any document over fifty pages seems a bit cumbersome because it just takes too long to move around the document and make the frequent saves necessary to protect the document.

In a long document, the pages appear on your screen one after another. Think of your document as a long scroll with lines marking the pages.

There is more than one way to break a page. If you've been experimenting on your own, you may have already created a second page by accidentally using WordPerfect's automatic page break feature.

Automatic Page Breaks

WordPerfect knows how many lines of text can fit on a page. It is a careful deduction of the paper size minus the margins (both set through the Format menu and covered in earlier chapters). The Ln amount in the lower left of the screen shows how many inches of the page have been filled with text up to your cursor position. On a typical 11-inch piece of paper with 1-inch top and bottom margins, you will be able to type to about the 9-inch mark before WordPerfect inserts a page break automatically for you. The exact measure varies according to the line spacing you're using (such as single or double) and the line height. (Both are set through the Format menu.) If you edit the page and add or delete lines of text, the page break remains at the same line. The text, in effect, "moves" to fill the page.

On your screen, an automatic page break appears as a dashed line, as shown in Figure 12-1. Notice that on the Reveal Code screen, the automatic page break is shown as [SPg] (soft page break). "Soft page break" is WordPerfectese for an automatically inserted page break. If you insert a page break manually, this is referred to as a "hard page break."

Creating a Manual Page Break

You'll often want a page break before WordPerfect enters one. For example, when you create a letter with several attachments, you may want to put the letter on the first page of the document and the attachments on subsequent pages, keeping all the related material in one WordPerfect document. When you print, you can insert letterhead for the first page and plain sheets after that.

Of course, you could press Enter enough times to take advantage of WordPerfect's automatic page break, but editing the text later could throw off the pages. Instead, use a manual (hard) page break.

```
File Edit Search Layout Mark Tools Font Graphics Help
                        Barbara J. Wiley
                        3421 Pecos Way
                    San Diego, California 92123


Experience:

---------------------------------------------------------------
    1988-present   Programmer     Barney Corporation, 4566
                                    Doc 1 Pg 2 Ln 9.83" Pos 1"
[   ▲    ▲    ▲    ▲    ▲    ▲    ▲    ▲    ▲    ▲   }   ▲    ▲
[Just:Full][HRt]
[HRt]
Experience:[HRt]
[HRt-SPg]
[Tab]1988[-]present[Tab]Programmer[+Indent]Barney Corporation, 4566[SRt]
Oakway, Austin, Texas 78759[SRt]
(512) 253[-]9900.[HRt]
[HRt]
[+Indent][+Indent][+Indent][+Indent][+Indent][+Indent][+Indent]Cobol and PL1 in
an IBM[SRt]

Press Reveal Codes to restore screen
```

Figure 12-1. Automatic page break

129

To manually break a page, put your cursor on the line and column where you want the page to be broken. Press Ctrl-Enter. A double dashed line like that shown in Figure 12-2 is inserted and the [HPg] (hard page break) code is inserted in your document. Text (if any) starting with the character your cursor is on appears after the manual page break. If you want to get rid of the manual page break, just delete the code.

Moving Between Pages

Once you have multiple pages, you will want to be able to move from page to page quickly. The number of the page appears in the bottom right corner of your screen. In this sample line

Doc 1 Pg 4 Ln 8" Pos 3"

your cursor is shown to be on page 4. To go directly to page 15, press Ctrl-Home Go to Page. This prompt appears:

Go to

```
File Edit Search Layout Mark Tools Font Graphics Help
_____

          Barbara J. Wiley


==================================================================


                       Barbara J. Wiley
                       3421 Pecos Way
                                          Doc 1 Pg 2 Ln 8.5" Pos 2"
   ▲   {   ▲   ▲   ▲   ▲   ▲   ▲   ▲   }   ▲   ▲   ▲   ▲
[HRt]
Barbara J. Wiley[HRt]
[HRt]
[HPg]
[HRt]
[HRt]
[L/R Mar:1",1"][Just:Center][Hyph Off]Barbara J. Wiley[HRt]
3421 Pecos Way[HRt]
San Diego, California 92123[HRt]
[Just:Full][HRt]

Press Reveal Codes to restore screen
```

Figure 12-2. Manual (hard) page break

Enter 15 and press Enter. Your cursor goes to the upper left corner of the first line of page 15.

To move only one page, press PgUp (to go up or "back" in the document) or PgDn (to go down or "forward" in the document). When you use either of these keys, you are taken to the upper left of the first line of that page.

Preventing Widows and Orphans

To many beginning users, the terms "widows" and "orphans" have to do with women who have lost their husbands and children who have lost their parents. In word processing, the terms have to do with losses too—specifically, a single line of a paragraph has been lost from the rest of its paragraph by being split off by a page break. A *widow* is the first line of a paragraph alone at the end of a page. An *orphan* is the last line of a paragraph isolated at the top of a page. Figure 12-3 shows a widow and an orphan.

If you don't like the appearance of widows and orphans, you can ask WordPerfect to prevent them. Press Shift-F8 Format then select 1 Line or select Line from the Layout menu.

From the Format: Line menu, select 9 Widow/Orphan Protection. Press *y* for Yes. Press F7 Exit until you return to your document. The code [W/O On] is placed in your text to indicate that widow/orphan protection is activated from that point forward in the document.

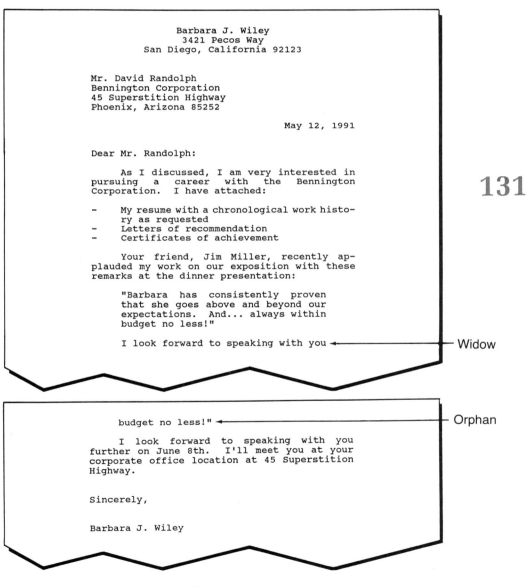

131

Figure 12-3. A widow and orphan

> ▶ **Hint:** To protect an entire document, place the widow/orphan code at the beginning of the document.

Q Widow/Orphan Protection

1. Put the cursor where you want protection to start. Press Shift-F8 Format and then select 1 Line or select Line from the Layout menu.

   The Format: Line menu appears.

2. Select 9 Widow/Orphan Protection, type *y*, and press F7 Exit to go back to your document.

   A code is inserted in your text.

   □

132

Conditional End of Page

Sometimes you will want to keep several lines together in a document. For example, in Figure 12-4, part of the resume is split by a soft page break automatically inserted by WordPerfect. The split is inappropriate. To keep the lines together, you could insert a manual page break above the lines. The problem with this is that if you edit text, the hard page break may end up cutting the page too short. A better solution is to enter a *conditional end of page*, which keeps together the number of lines you specify so they can't be split between pages.

First, identify how many lines you want to keep together. In our example, we'll keep the resume entry together (four lines). Then, place the cursor in the line above those lines you want to keep together. Press Shift-F8 Format and then *4* Other or select Other from the Layout menu. From the Format: Other menu, select 2 Conditional End of Page. This prompt appears:

Number of Lines to Keep Together:

Type in the number of lines to keep together and press Enter. The code [Cndl EOP:4] appears, indicating that four pages are

```
File Edit Search Layout Mark Tools Font Graphics Help
─────────────────────────────────────────────────────────
                               Oakway, Austin, Texas 78759
                               (512) 253-9900.

                               Cobol and PL1 in an IBM
                               environment.

     1985-1988.      Operator  Beverly World, PO Box 843,
                               Austin, Texas 78778
                               (512) 435-9000.


Education:

     Bachelors of Science (Computer Science)
     University of Iowa, Iowa City, Iowa.
     ──────────────────────────────────────────────────────
     Awarded 1984.

Affiliations:

     Data Processing Professional Group.  1985-present.

                              Doc 1 Pg 3 Ln 7.5" Pos 4.5"
```

133

Figure 12-4. Resume lines split by soft page break

to be kept together. The text that was split is automatically
moved past the page break. Figure 12-5 shows the resume after

```
File Edit Search Layout Mark Tools Font Graphics Help
─────────────────────────────────────────────────────────

─────────────────────────────────────────────────────────
Education:

     Bachelors of Science (Computer Science)
     University of Iowa, Iowa City, Iowa.
     Awarded 1984.

Affiliations:
                              Doc 1 Pg 3 Ln 9.17" Pos 1"
[   ▲   ▲    ▲    ▲    ▲    ▲    ▲    ▲    ▲    }   ▲    ▲
Austin, Texas 78778[HRt]
[→Indent][→Indent][→Indent][→Indent][→Indent][→Indent][→Indent](512) 435[-]9000.
[HRt]
[HRt]
[Cnd1 EOP:6][HRt-SPg]
Education:[HRt]
[HRt]
[Tab]Bachelors of Science (Computer Science)[HRt]
[Tab]University of Iowa, Iowa City, Iowa. [HRt]
[Tab]Awarded 1984.[HRt]

Press Reveal Codes to restore screen
```

*Figure 12-5. Resume lines after inserting conditional end
of page*

the conditional end of page has been inserted. Notice the code placement.

Ⓠ Entering a Conditional End of Page

1. Identify the number of lines to keep together and place the cursor before the first line.

   The lines after the cursor will be affected.

2. Press Shift-F8 Format and select 4 Other or select Other on the Layout menu.

   The Format: Other menu appears.

3. Select 2 Conditional End of Page, type in the number of lines to be kept together, and press Enter.

   The lines are kept together on a page.

Block Protect

You may want to keep a given block of text together (versus specifying a particular number of lines). If so, use the *block protect* feature instead of the conditional end of page. With block protect, you can change the number of lines in the block through editing and the block will remain together on a single page.

This feature is especially useful for tables or any block that may be edited to a different number of lines. For example, Figure 12-6 shows text in a block protect. The entire block was moved to the start of a page. Notice the [BlockPro:On] and [BlockPro:Off] codes that mark the beginning and end of the block.

▶ **Hint:** Since the text you are block protecting is to be placed on one page, you cannot block protect more than a pageful of text.

To start, block the text using Alt-F4 Block. The blocked text is highlighted. Press Shift-F8 Format. Instead of getting the Format menu, this message appears:

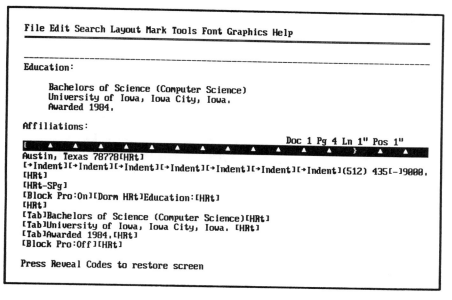

File Edit Search Layout Mark Tools Font Graphics Help

```
Education:

      Bachelors of Science (Computer Science)
      University of Iowa, Iowa City, Iowa.
      Awarded 1984.

Affiliations:
                                          Doc 1 Pg 4 Ln 1" Pos 1"
[   ▲    ▲    ▲    ▲    ▲    ▲    ▲    ▲   ▲    }   ▲    ▲
Austin, Texas 78778[HRt]
[→Indent][→Indent][→Indent][→Indent][→Indent][→Indent][→Indent](512) 435[−]9000.
[HRt]
[HRt−SPg]
[Block Pro:On][Dorm HRt]Education:[HRt]
[HRt]
[Tab]Bachelors of Science (Computer Science)[HRt]
[Tab]University of Iowa, Iowa City, Iowa, [HRt]
[Tab]Awarded 1984,[HRt]
[Block Pro:Off][HRt]

Press Reveal Codes to restore screen
```

Figure 12-6. Block protected text

Protect block? (Y/N) No

Press *y* for Yes and the block protection codes are inserted into the document.

Q Block Protection

1. Block the text with Alt-F4 Block.

   The blocked text is highlighted.

2. Press Shift-F8 Format and type *y* for Yes.

   The block protection codes are inserted.

Summary

In this chapter you've learned:

▶ WordPerfect automatically inserts soft page breaks at the end of the page.

▶ You may press Ctrl-Enter to place a hard page break in your text.

▶ Use Ctrl-Home Go To, PgUp, and PgDn to quickly move between pages.

▶ Use widow/orphan protection to stop single lines of a paragraph from splitting to a new page (select Line on the Layout menu).

▶ Use conditional end of page to keep a number of lines together on a page (select Other from the Layout menu).

▶ Use block protection to keep a block of text together. After blocking the text, press Shift-F8 Format and respond to the prompts.

136

Chapter 13

Page Numbers

In This Chapter

► *How to add page numbers*
► *How to suppress page numbers*
► *How to add a page number in the body of the text*

Page Number Choices

Numbering pages is handy for short documents and essential for most long documents. But don't tediously number each page in the document by hand. Instead, have WordPerfect automatically number your pages. WordPerfect allows you to select the:

► New page number (including the number with which to start consecutive numbering) and the type—roman or arabic
► Style (number alone, or accompanied by text)
► Position of the number on the page

You may change these options on any page you like and as often as you like in a document. A new code is inserted each time you enter page numbering options. The code affects the page on which it is entered and all following text until a new code is encountered.

> ⊘ **Caution:** Place the codes controlling page numbering at the top of a page. If you put text before the page codes, the page numbers may not print as you anticipated. If you accidentally put conflicting page numbering codes on a page, the pages won't number as you anticipated.

First, we'll cover each of the page numbering options, and then we'll step through the "how to" of setting up page numbers.

The New Page Number

"New Page Number" is WordPerfect's option to allow you to select the page number you want to start with at a given point in the document along with the type of number. The type may be roman (type *I* or *i*) or arabic (type *1*).

For example, you might have several WordPerfect documents making up one long, printed document. The first three pages of the first document are an introduction numbered i, ii, and iii, and the next 15 pages in the document may be numbered 1 through 15. You then would want the first WordPerfect page of the second document to be numbered as page 16 with consecutive numbering continuing from there.

As you can see from this example, you can start new page numbering (number and type) at the start of a document or on any page. The page number you've assigned is displayed in the bottom right of the screen.

You have three type choices. You can choose lowercase roman numerals:

i, ii, iii, iv, and so on.

Second, you can pick uppercase roman numerals:

I, II, III, IV, and so on.

Third (and most often), you may use arabic numbers:

1, 2, 3, 4, and so on.

Arabic is WordPerfect's default.

When you enter a new page number, a code like this appears in your document: [Pg Num:4] with the number identifying the new starting number. This number is displayed in the type (roman or arabic) you've chosen.

Style of Text/Page Number

The "Page Number Style" is WordPerfect's option to allow you to enter the page number alone or to enter text along with the page number. As an example, you may want the first three pages of a document to have this text along with the page number:

        Appendix A—Page 1
        Appendix A—Page 2
        Appendix A—Page 3

On the fourth page, you may want to change to the following style and continue it through the rest of the document:

        Appendix B—Page 1

"Appendix A—Page" is the common style in this example, followed by WordPerfect's insertion of the "New Page Number" (the actual number and type of number) you've identified.
    The text here (Appendix) is just one way to use the page number style feature with text and symbols. (You can enter any text up to thirty characters.) For instance, you may want to insert a date:

        June 10, 1988 ---- (1)

a copyright notice:

        (c) 1989 Walden Co. / Pg 1

the author's name:

        By Jeffery K. Cochran p. #1

a confidential notification:

        CONFIDENTIAL: 1

139

identify the document as a draft:

!!!! D R A F T !!!! p. 1

or just add a decoration to the page number:

******** 1 ********

The text and page number appear when the document is printed.

> ▶ **Note:** You may need to enter more then thirty charac- ters along with a page number. If so, check out the discussion of headers and footers in Chapter 20.

When you set the style in WordPerfect, you enter the text along with a symbol (^B—entered by pressing Ctrl-B) for the page number. If the page number is to appear at the end of the text instead of within text, you can just enter the text (include a space if appropriate) and WordPerfect will automatically enter the ^B for you.

> ⊘ **Caution:** Press Ctrl and B simultaneously. *Do not* press a caret (^) and a B. If you do, the caret and B will print in place of the desired page number.

When you enter a new page number style, this type of code is placed in the document:

`[Pg Num Style: Confidential Draft/Page ^B]`

The complete text of the style appears, along with ^B, which symbolizes the position of the page number.

Position on the Page

When it comes to positioning the page number, you are offered a variety of selections. Figure 13-1 illustrates the options. As shown in the figure, you can place the page number in the top left, top center, top right, bottom left, bottom center, or bottom right. The numbers in the "Every Page" diagram are simply identifiers for the position you can select. Look at the "Alternating Pages" diagram in the figure. If you are printing pages that will be copied double sided, you can enter the page number on the upper "outside" of the page or the lower "outside" of the page.

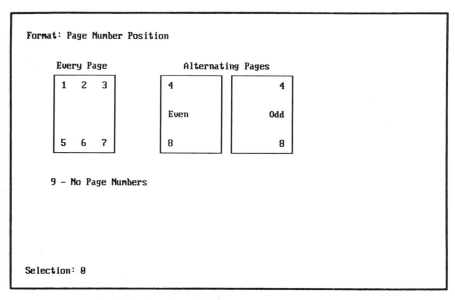

Figure 13-1. Possible page number positions

141

Also notice in Figure 13-1 that you may select "No Page Number." You can skip page numbers for one or more pages.

Once you add a position for a page number, a code like this appears in the document:

```
[Pg Numbering:Bottom Center]
```

The location of the page number is clearly shown.

How to Add a Page Number

Now that you know *what* you can do, *how* do you do it? Here are the steps. Place your cursor (before any existing text) at the top left of the page where you want page numbering to begin. Press Shift-F8 and select 2 Page or select Page from the Layout menu. Select 6 Page Numbering. The Format: Page Numbering menu appears (see Figure 13-2).

```
Format: Page Numbering

    1 - New Page Number        4

    2 - Page Number Style      ^B

    3 - Insert Page Number

    4 - Page Number Position No page numbering





Selection: 0
```

Figure 13-2. The Format: Page Numbering menu

To enter the number of the page to use and the type of number (arabic or roman), select *1* New Page Number. Enter the page number in arabic or roman style and press Enter.

To enter text before, after, or around the page number, select *2* Page Number Style. Type in the text and enter ^B (Ctrl- B) to position the page number. If you don't enter Ctrl-B, WordPerfect inserts the page number at the end of the text. Press Enter when you are done.

Select the positioning of the page number (or no page number) by choosing 4 Page Number Position. The diagram shown in Figure 13-1 appears. Select a page position by entering a number 1 through 8 and press Enter.

Once you have entered all the desired selections, press F7 Exit until you are returned to your document. You may want to check the Reveal Codes screen to ensure that all the selections are as you desired. The page numbers will *not* appear on your page; they only appear when the document is printed.

If you have graphics capabilities, you can view the page numbers on your screen by using Shift-F7 Print and then selecting 6 View Document. Try your computer to see it has this capability. If it does not, a message will appear. If it does, a screen like that shown in Figure 13-3 will appear.

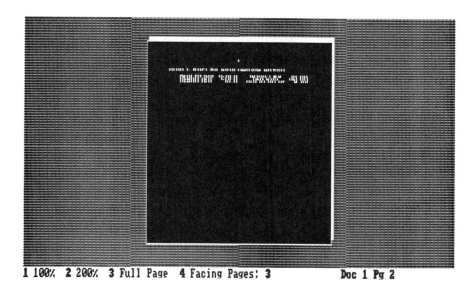

1 100%   2 200%   3 Full Page   4 Facing Pages: 3   Doc 1 Pg 2

Figure 13-3. Page numbers appear with View Document

Q Page Numbering

1. Place your cursor at the top of a page and press Shift-F8 Format then *2* Page or select Page from the Layout menu.

   The Format: Page menu appears.

2. Select *6* Page Numbering.

   The Format: Page Numbering menu appears.

3. Select among the options according to the page numbering you want; press F7 Exit when you are done.

   Codes are placed in your documents and the page numbers appear when the document is printed. □

Suppressing Page Numbers

You may want to suppress a page number on one page. This is sometimes required if you want to place a large graphic on a page or give a different look to the page. When you suppress the page number on a page, that page number is omitted from the consecutive count. For example, if you suppress the page number on page 3, the pages will be numbered 1, 2, (page 3 will have no page number), 4, 5, and so on.

To suppress a page number, press Shift-F8 Format and select 2 Page or select Page from the Layout menu. From the Format: Page menu, select 8 Suppress (this page only). The Format: Suppress (this page only) menu appears (see Figure 13-4). Select 4 Suppress Page Numbering and enter a *y* for Yes. Press F7 Exit until you return to your document. The [Suppress:PgNum] code is placed in your document.

144

```
Format: Suppress (this page only)

    1 - Suppress All Page Numbering, Headers and Footers

    2 - Suppress Headers and Footers

    3 - Print Page Number at Bottom Center    No

    4 - Suppress Page Numbering              No

    5 - Suppress Header A                    No

    6 - Suppress Header B                    No

    7 - Suppress Footer A                    No

    8 - Suppress Footer B                    No




Selection: 0
```

Figure 13-4. Format: Suppress menu

To suppress the numbers on several pages, follow the procedure to add a page number and select No Page Numbers for the Page Number Position. Then add them when you want page numbers again.

Inserting the Page Number in the Body of the Page

For reference purposes, you may want to insert the page number in the body of the text. These phrases illustrate several examples:

```
Return to this page (page 3) when you have completed the test.
The instructions follow (pg 4).
```

Use WordPerfect's feature for inserting page numbers (instead of typing in the page number yourself). That way, if the number of the page changes due to editing, the number that prints will always be correct.

To enter the page number, position your cursor in the body of the text where the number is to appear. Press Shift-F8 Format and select 2 Page or select Page from the Layout menu. Select 6 Page Numbering. From the Format: Page Numbering menu select 3 Insert Page Number. You are returned to your document and the ^B symbol appears in the document. This symbol will be replaced with the page number when the document prints. You can see the full code [Insert Pg Num:^B] with the Reveal Codes screen.

145

Summary

In this chapter you've learned:

► That you may enter a new page number in roman or arabic style anywhere in a document. Subsequent page numbers will be consecutively numbered.

► You may enter text along with the page number.

► You may select from several different page positions for the page number.

► To add page numbers, stop page numbering, or add a page number in the body of the text, start with Shift-F8 Format, then select 2 Page (or Page from the Layout menu) and 6 Page Numbering. Finally, complete the options.

► To suppress a page number on a single page use Shift-F8 Format and then 2 Page (or Page from the Layout menu). Select 8 Suppress and then 4 Suppress Page Numbering.

146

Giving Characters a New Look

In This Chapter

► *How to change the size of a character*
► *Ways to change the appearance of a character*
► *What fonts are and how to change them*

New Look Possibilities

Characters donning a new look can add emphasis, interest, and clarity to your documents. Some looks can also be used to aid in the editing process. For example, Figure 14-1 shows our résumé before a new look is applied. Figure 14-2 shows the same résumé after some of WordPerfect's character-enhancement features were used.

What character enhancement is possible depends not only on WordPerfect but on your printer as well. Not all printers are capable of printing all of WordPerfect's character options. You can experiment with your printer to see which results are possible for you.

```
                        Barbara J. Wiley
                         3421 Pecos Way
                   San Diego, California 92123


     Experience:

         1988-present   Programmer      Barney Corporation, 4566
                                        Oakway, Austin, Texas 78759
                                        (512) 253-9900.

                                        Cobol and PL1 in an IBM
                                        environment.

         1985-1988      Operator        Beverly World, PO Box 843,
                                        Austin, Texas 78778
                                        (512) 435-9000.

     Education:

         Bachelors of Science (Computer Science)
         University of Iowa, Iowa City, Iowa.
         Awarded 1984.

     Affiliations:

         Data Processing Professional Group.   1985 to present.
```

148

Figure 14-1. The resume "before"

```
                        Barbara J. Wiley
                         3421 Pecos Way
                   San Diego, California 92123


     Experience:

         1988-present   Programmer      Barney Corporation, 4566
                                        Oakway, Austin, Texas 78759
                                        (512) 253-9900.

                                        Cobol and PL1 in an IBM
                                        environment.

         1985-1988      Operator        Beverly World, PO Box 843,
                                        Austin, Texas 78778
                                        (512) 435-9000.

     Education:

         Bachelors of Science (Computer Science)
         University of Iowa, Iowa City, Iowa.
         Awarded 1984.

     Affiliations:

         Data Processing Professional Group.   1985 to present.
```

Figure 14-2. The resume "after"

Fonts

You will use WordPerfect's Font feature to control the look of characters. For our purposes, *font* refers to the size and appearance of the characters. With Font, you can control the height, width, placement, boldness, and style of characters.

Controlling Character Size

Several of the options for controlling character size and position are shown in Figure 14-3. These include:

▶ *Superscript*: Superscripted characters are placed somewhat above the line of normal text. Superscripted text is often used for footnotes and formulas. Most printers are capable of printing superscripted text.

▶ *Subscript*: Subscripted characters are placed slightly lower than the line of text. Formulas often require subscripted text. Common printers handle this option.

▶ *Fine/Small/Large/Very large/Extra large*: The size of the characters can vary from fine to extra large. Many printers cannot handle this option. Others handle it, but produce unexpected results.

149

```
Superscript:  See footnotes below.[2]

Subscript:    H₂O is in abundant supply.

Small:        Always read the small print.
```

Figure 14-3. Font sizes

To use size, block (Alt-F4) the text that you want to appear in the desired font size. Go to the font size options by pressing Ctrl-F8 Font then *1* Size or by selecting the Font menu. Select the font size you want. Codes reflecting your selection are placed in your document on either side of the blocked text. These are the codes:

```
[SUPRSCPT]your text[suprscpt]
[SUBSCPT]your text[subscpt]
[FINE]your text[fine]
```

```
[SMALL]your text[small]
[LARGE]your text[large]
[VRY LARGE]your text[vry large]
[EXT LARGE]your text[ext large]
```

　　　You can apply a size choice to a single character or a whole document. You can also apply more than one size choice to text; for example, you could superscript small text.

　　　Once you apply a size choice, the text will not look different on your screen. The size is applied when the text is printed (assuming, of course, that your printer handles the size).

Font Size Selection

150

1. Use Alt-F4 to block the text you want to affect.

   The text is highlighted.

2. Press Ctrl-F8 Font and *1* Size or select the Font menu. Select the size.

   Codes are placed in your document before and after the blocked text.

Altering the Appearance of Characters

WordPerfect's appearance options have something for everyone. Figure 14-4 shows some of the appearance options you may select (each is described later in this section).

Bold

Underline

Double underline

Shadow

SMALL CAPS

Redline

Strikeout

Figure 14-4. Appearances

　　　The process for entering an appearance is similar to that for entering a size. Use Alt-F4 Block to block the text you want to affect. Press Ctrl-F8 Font and type *2* Appearance or select the Font menu, then Appearance. Check the printer manual to make sure your printer handles the appearance you want to choose. Select the appearance desired. Codes are placed around the text. The text may not look different on your screen.

Q **Character Appearance Selection**

1. Use Alt-F4 to block the text you want to affect.

   The text is highlighted.

2. Press Ctrl-F8 Font and *2* Appearance or select Appearance from the Font menu. Select the appearance.

   Codes are placed in your document before and after the text block.

As with making size choices, you can combine appearances and sizes with appearances. Just apply the necessary selections. The appearances are:

151

▶ *Bold*: Bold text is darker and wider than normal text. Usually, bold text will be displayed on your screen as brighter or in a different color than other text. Use bold for emphasis. The codes placed around the blocked text are [BOLD][bold].

▶ *Underline*: Text may be printed with a single underline. (You cannot type in text and then use the underline key to underline it unless you block the text first.) The codes are: [UND][und].

▶ *Double underline*: Text may be printed with two underlines. Some printers do not handle this option. If your printer does, it can give your documents an unusual touch. These codes are placed around the text: [DBL UND][dbl und].

▶ *Italic*: If your printer handles italic text, you can introduce a typeset quality to your documents. Use it sparingly to emphasize key words or phrases. Use it throughout invitations or announcements to give them an elegant appearance. The [ITALC][italc] codes surround the affected text.

▶ *Outline*: This special style is useful as an attention-getter, although many printers do not handle the style. The codes are [OUTLN][outln].

▶ *Shadow*: This creates a shadow effect by offsetting a character from itself. Shadow is effective for use in flyers and advertisements. The codes are [SHADW][shadw].

▶ *Small Caps*: Regardless of whether you enter the text in upper- or lowercase letters, the text is printed in small uppercase (capital) letters. On the Reveal Codes screen, the codes [SM CAP][sm cap] appear.

▶ *Redline*: This appearance is often used to display edits that should be reviewed. Text to be added can be shown in redline. The codes are [REDLN][redln].

▶ *Strikeout*: When showing edits made to a document, you can use strikeout to illustrate text to be removed. The codes [STKOUT][stkout] are used.

152

Redline and strikeout come with a nifty bonus. When you use them (usually to illustrate edits to a document), you can automatically strip them from your document. The editing process goes like this:

1. Enter text to be inserted in redline and text to be deleted in strikeout.

2. Review the text as it will be edited. Delete any redlined text that you decide you don't want inserted. Type in (using normal text) any stricken text that you decide to retain. This way, when you apply the automatic removal of the marks, you get the intended effect.

3. Automatically remove the redline marks (the text stays) and the strikeout text (the text is deleted). To do this, press Alt-F5 Mark Text and type *6* Generate or select Generate from the Mark menu. Press *1* Remove Redline Markings and Strikeout Text from Document. Type *y* at the "Delete" question in order to remove the redline appearance and delete the text marked with strikeout.

The two most popular WordPerfect appearances are bold and underline. Because of their popularity, special keys are assigned to streamline their choice. For entering bold, press F6 Bold. To enter underline, press F8 Underline. In both cases, the codes are inserted in your document. If you block text before pressing the key, the blocked text will be affected. If you press either key without first blocking text, the relevant codes are placed around your cursor location and any text you subsequently type will be bold or underlined. Type in the text, and then move your cursor one space beyond the ending code.

▶ **Hint:** This same approach for entering new text can be used with either size or appearance. To enter a size or appearance and then the text, select the size or appearance, type in the text, and move the cursor beyond the closing code.

Selecting Fonts

Some printers have specific type font capabilities. As an example, Figure 14-5 illustrates our resume printed with the headings in the Helvetica font and the body in the Times Roman font.

153

Barbara J. Wiley
3421 Pecos Way
San Diego, California 92123

Experience:

1988-present	Programmer	Barney Corporation, 4566 Oakway, Austin, Texas 78759 (512) 253-9900.
		Cobol and PL1 in an IBM environment.
1985-1988	Operator	Beverly World, PO Box 843, Austin, Texas 78778 (512) 435-9000.

Education:

Bachelors of Science (Computer Science)
University of Iowa, Iowa City, Iowa.
Awarded 1984.

Affiliations:

Data Processing Professional Group. 1985 to present.

Figure 14-5. Helvetica and Times Roman fonts

To see which fonts are available for the printer you have currently selected, press Ctrl-F8 Font then *4* Base Font or select Base Font from the Font menu. A Base Font menu like that shown in Figure 14-6 appears. This menu displays the fonts available for your printer. To select a font, highlight the name of the font and type *1* Select. A code for the font is placed in your text and the text after that code is affected. You can change fonts as often as you like.

154

```
Base Font

    Courier 10cpi
    Courier 10cpi Bold
    Helv 14.4pt Bold (B)
    Line Draw 10cpi (Full)
    Line Printer 16.67cpi
    TmsRmn  8pt (B)
  * TmsRmn 10pt (B)
    TmsRmn 10pt Bold (B)
    TmsRmn 10pt Italic (B)




1 Select; N Name search: 1
```

Figure 14-6. Base Font menu

 New Font Selection

1. Place your cursor where the new font should take effect.

   Text after this point will be effected.

2. Press Ctrl-F8 Font and *4* Base Font or select Base Font from the Font menu.

   The Base Font menu appears with the possible fonts.

3. Highlight the font and type *1* Select.

   A code for the font is placed in the document. □

Summary

In this chapter you've learned:

▶ To change the size or appearance of characters, press Ctrl-F8 Font or select the Font menu. Continue making selections according to how you want your document to look.

▶ To change fonts, press Ctrl-F8 Font and 4 Base Font or select Base Font from the Font menu. Highlight the font and press 1 Select.

▶ Not all printers handle all fonts, sizes, and appearances. Experiment with your printer to determine its capabilities.

155

Chapter 15

Checking Your Spelling

In This Chapter

▶ *How to check the spelling of a single word, a page, a block of text, or a document*

▶ *How to use dictionaries*

▶ *How to count the number of words in a document*

What Is Spell Checking?

Don't reach for that dictionary! Instead, use WordPerfect's spell checker. With it, you can check the spelling of a single word, a page, or an entire document. WordPerfect locates its built-in dictionary, looks up any unrecognized word, and suggests alternative spellings—more than any paper dictionary suggests.

Not every word that WordPerfect identifies is misspelled. WordPerfect matches the words in your document with those in its dictionary. If a match is not found, the word is identified. Some words may be properly spelled but not in WordPerfect's dictionary: some professional jargon and proper names, for example, are not included. You can add words to the dictionary, however, to accommodate unusual words you commonly use.

> ⊘ **Caution:** Just because a document spell checks okay does not mean your document is free from typographical or editorial errors. For example, this sentence would pass WordPerfect's spell checker with flying colors: "I never seen him be long to a group before." Though you wouldn't want to be identified as the author of that sentence, the words it comprises are correctly spelled. Remember, even when using spell check, you still need to carefully proofread documents to check sentence structure and appropriate use of words.

In addition to checking the spelling of words, WordPerfect finds double occurrences of a word, a common typographical error. In this sentence, the word "the" was entered twice: "Politics is a risky business for the the faint of heart." If you were to spell check a document containing this sentence, WordPerfect would point out the redundant word and enable you to fix the sentence.

WordPerfect also identifies double capital letters at the beginning of a word (JUst) as well as a small then capital letter (jUst).

> ▶ **Hint:** Spell check the document when it is complete. Don't spell check a document early in development. You will just have to spell check it again after you edit it.

Correcting a Word, a Page, a Block, or a Document

To begin the spell check, place your cursor on the word, the page, or anywhere in the document you want to check in entirety. If you want to spell check a block of text, use Alt-F4 to block the appropriate text. Blocking text is useful when you've already spell checked a document, then edited a section, and now want to spell check only that edited section.

Press Ctrl-F2 Spell or select Spell from the Tools menu. If you are checking a word, page, or document, this menu appears at the bottom of the screen. (If you are checking a block, the spell check begins as soon as you delineate the block.)

`Check: 1 Word; 2 Page; 3 Document; 4 New Sup. Dictionary; 5 Look Up;`
`6 Count:`

To spell check a word, type *1* Word. To check the page your cursor is on, type *2* Page. To check the entire document, type *3* Document.

The spell check begins. WordPerfect skips those words that match words in the dictionary. When WordPerfect hits a word that is not in the dictionary, a screen like that shown in Figure 15-1 appears. The word identified as "misspelled" is highlighted. This screen suggests spelling alternatives and prompts you for the possible actions to take.

Select from these actions:

A-X Pick a letter of the suggested word to substitute for the misspelled word.

  1 Skip Once: Type *1* to skip this first occurrence of a "misspelling." An example might be a proper noun like "Tyme" that you want to change the next time it appears.

  2 Skip: Type *2* to skip all occurrences of the spelling. In this case, "Tyme" would be skipped throughout the document.

  3 Add: Type *3* to add the word to the dictionary. Future occurrences of this word will be skipped in this and any other document you spell check. Adding your own name to the dictionary is a good use of this feature.

  4 Edit: If you don't like the alternatives WordPerfect presents, you may edit the word (or any part of the document, for that matter). When you type *4* to edit, your cursor goes to the document. Make your changes and then press F7 Exit in order to go back to spell checking. If the word is still not recognized, it will be checked again.

  5 Look Up: To look up a different word, type *5*. This message appears:

`Word or word pattern:`

Type in the word (or a close likeness) and press Enter. The word you enter is checked.

159

6 Ignore Numbers: WordPerfect stops on unusual number combinations. To skip words with numbers in this document, type *6*.

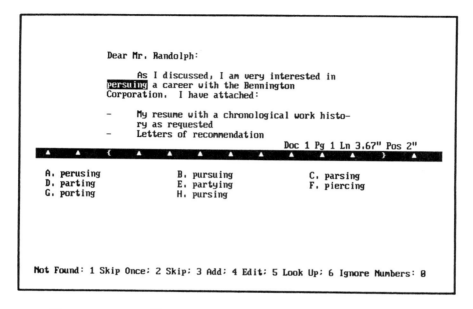

Dear Mr. Randolph:

    As I discussed, I am very interested in **persuing** a career with the Bennington Corporation. I have attached:

    —   My resume with a chronological work history as requested
    —   Letters of recommendation

        Doc 1 Pg 1 Ln 3.67" Pos 2"

A. perusing   B. pursuing   C. parsing
D. parting   E. partying   F. piercing
G. porting   H. pursing

Not Found: 1 Skip Once: 2 Skip; 3 Add; 4 Edit; 5 Look Up; 6 Ignore Numbers: 0

Figure 15-1. Spelling alternatives

Figure 15-2 shows an example of a double word. If WordPerfect encounters double words, these options are available:

2 Skip: Type *2* to skip the double occurrence.
3 Delete 2nd: Type *3* to delete the second occurrence of the word.
4 Edit: Type *4* to edit the text.
5 Disable Double Word Checking: Type *5* to stop finding double words in this spell check session.

Figure 15-3 shows a capitalization problem. When WordPerfect comes across a word with the first two letters or just the second letter capitalized (JUst or jUst), these options come up:

2 Skip: Type *2* to skip the word.
3 Replace: Type *3* to change to the same word having only the first letter capitalized.

4 Edit: Type *4* to edit the text.
5 Disable Case Checking: Type *5* to stop locating case problems.

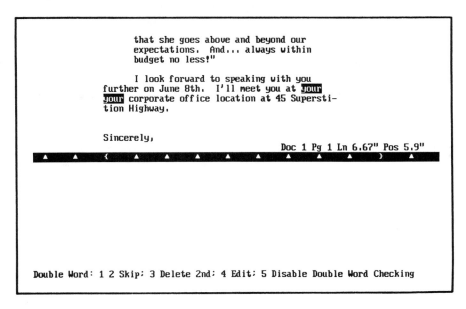

that she goes above and beyond our
expectations. And... always within
budget no less!"

I look forward to speaking with you
further on June 8th. I'll meet you at your
your corporate office location at 45 Superstition Highway.

Sincerely,

Doc 1 Pg 1 Ln 6.67" Pos 5.9"

Double Word: 1 2 Skip; 3 Delete 2nd; 4 Edit; 5 Disable Double Word Checking

Figure 15-2. Double word

When you have finished spell checking, a message identifies the number of words checked. As the message says, press any key to go back to your document.

Word count: 234 Press any key to continue

When you check spelling, case is ignored by WordPerfect. When a word is substituted, the case of the original word is followed. Figure 15-4 shows the case of a word identified as misspelled and Figure 15-5 illustrates the case after the substitution is made. Notice that the case remains the same.

 Note: If you are using the spell checker and want to quit, just press F1 Cancel.

161

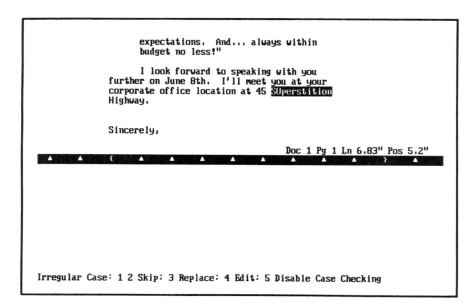

Figure 15-3. Capitalization

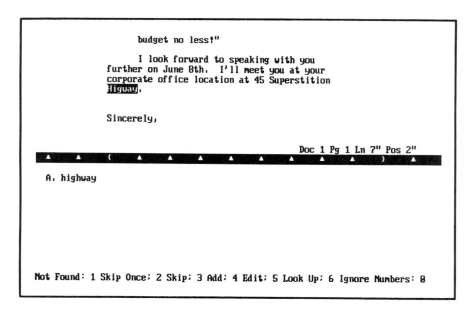

Figure 15-4. Case before substitution

162

```
    "Barbara has consistently proven
    that she goes above and beyond our
    expectations.  And... always within
    budget no less!"

        I look forward to speaking with you
    further on June 8th.  I'll meet you at your
    corporate office location at 45 Superstition
    Highway.


    Sincerely,


    Barbara J. Wiley


=================================================================================
                    Barbara J. Wiley
                    3421 Pecos Way
               San Diego, California 92123

Experience:

Check: 1 Word; 2 Page; 3 Document; 4 New Sup. Dictionary; 5 Look Up; 6 Count: 0
```

163

Figure 15-5. Case after substitution

Q Spell Check

1. Block the text if you wish, or place the cursor on the word, page, or document you wish to check.

   You have identified the text to spell check.

2. Press Ctrl-F2 Spell or select Spell from the Tools menu.

   If you are checking a word, page, or document (as opposed to a text block), a menu line appears at the bottom of the screen.

3. Select the amount of text to check (1 Word, 2 Page, or 3 Document).

   The first unrecognized word is found.

4. Replace the word or make another selection.

   Your selection is carried out. Spell checking continues.

Creating Supplemental Dictionaries

When you add a word to the dictionary, it is saved in a file named WP{WP}US.SUP. As you add words, you are creating a personal supplemental dictionary. To do so, press Ctrl-F2 Spell and select *4* New Sup. Dictionary. Then enter a path and name to identify the dictionary you are using with this document. This feature enables you to create more than one supplemental dictionary. You could, for example, have a supplemental dictionary for legal terms, one for medical terms, and so on.

Looking Up a Word

164

You can look up a word as you work. Press Ctrl-F2 Spell or select Spell from the Tools menu. Pick *5* Look Up, type in the word to look up, and continue as you would with any spell check procedure.

Counting Words

You can count the words in a document with the spell checker as well, regardless of whether you want to spell check the document. This is useful for writers who have a given length in mind. Just press Ctrl-F2 Spell or select Spell from the Tools menu. Type *6* Count and the spell checker counts the words in the document and displays the total.

Summary

In this chapter you've learned:

▶ To check the spelling of a single word, a page, or a document, position the cursor and press Ctrl-F2 Spell or select Spell from the Tools menu. Choose the amount of text you want to check.

▶ To check the spelling in a block of text, block the text with Alt-F4 block before using Spell.

▶ To add words to a supplemental dictionary, select 4 New Supplemental Dictionary from the Spell options and enter the path and name of the dictionary.

▶ To count words in a document (and not spell check) select 6 Count from the Spell options.

165

Controlling Your Documents

In This Chapter

▶ *How to copy documents*
▶ *How to delete documents*
▶ *How to move or rename documents*
▶ *How to save and use documents in other formats*

Managing Documents with the List Files Screen

When you start using WordPerfect, you'll have only a few documents stored on a disk. Managing them should not be too important since you can probably locate most of the documents and remember their contents. But as you create more and more documents, managing them increases in importance. You will have many documents on many disks; just locating the document you want can be a problem. Additionally, some documents may become damaged or lost. For these reasons, it is important to have a system of managing your documents.

One useful technique is to keep related documents on disks. For example, you might have a disk of letters, a disk of documents created for a year-end report, and a disk of documents for a system design. Using your disks as "file cabinets" will help you find documents easily.

It is also important to follow a scheme of naming documents so you can readily identify them. If, after creating several documents, you think of a better naming scheme, go ahead and rename the documents. Another important management task is to delete unnecessary documents so you can more easily locate the useful documents.

This chapter covers speedy methods to manipulate files in order to manage them.

Accessing the List Files Screen

The List Files screen can't be beat when it comes to handling document management activities. Go to this screen by pressing F5 List Files or by selecting List Files from the file menu. A prompt like this appears:

```
Dir C:\WP51\DOC\*.*
```

Type in the drive, path, and file identifier desired. (For example, you could type A:*.WPP to display all the files on the disk in drive A that have the .WPP extension.) Press Enter and you are taken to the List Files screen shown in Figure 16-1.

What the List Files Screen Tells You

Starting at the top of the List Files screen, you are given this information:

▶ *Date and time*: Always make sure your computer records the correct date and time. If you have more than one version of a document, the date and time might be the only way to identify the most recent version. The date and time is automatically assigned to a document when you save it. Most computers have a clock that automatically enters the date and time for you.

```
11-19-89  07:22p            Directory C:\WP51\DOC\*.WPP
Document size:      378   Free: 14,112,768 Used:     707,302    Files:      72

   .   Current    <Dir>              ..   Parent    <Dir>
1-5      .WPP        884  01-01-80 12:11a  BELET    .WPP    1,081  01-01-80 01:15a
BELET10E.WPP      1,533  10-29-89 10:05p  BELET111.WPP    2,660  11-12-89 10:05p
BELET112.WPP      2,660  11-12-89 10:05p  BELET141.WPP    3,409  11-12-89 10:23p
BELET142.WPP      3,481  11-12-89 10:22p  BELET145.WPP    4,205  11-12-89 10:40p
BELET15E.WPP      4,205  11-12-89 10:46p  BELET41  .WPP      519  10-22-89 09:08a
BELET42 .WPP        561  10-22-89 09:11a  BELET45  .WPP      568  10-22-89 01:20p
BELET53 .WPP        788  10-28-89 02:20p  BELET76  .WPP      967  10-22-89 09:33p
BELET84 .WPP        984  10-22-89 09:45p  BENLET   .WPP    2,062  01-01-80 01:12a
BENLET11.WPP        831  01-01-80 01:09a  FIG10-5  .WPP      978  01-01-80 01:09a
FIG143  .WPP        922  11-12-89 10:29p  FIG144   .WPP    3,416  11-12-89 10:33p
WPF1    .WPP     13,707  10-28-89 03:18p  WPF1-50  .WPP   13,706  10-28-89 03:04p
WPF1-AS .WPP     12,541  10-28-89 03:05p  WPF10    .WPP   10,849  10-29-89 10:02p
WPF10-50.WPP     10,849  10-29-89 10:02p  WPF10-AS.WPP    9,553  10-29-89 10:03p
WPF11   .WPP     14,922  01-01-80 07:09a  WPF11-50.WPP   14,922  01-01-80 07:09a
WPF11-AS.WPP     13,659  01-01-80 07:10a  WPF12    .WPP   11,767  01-01-80 01:45p
WPF12-50.WPP     11,767  01-01-80 01:45p  WPF12-AS.WPP   10,566  01-01-80 01:46p
WPF13   .WPP     13,206  01-01-80 04:13a  WPF13-50.WPP   13,206  01-01-80 04:13a
WPF13-AS.WPP     11,973  01-01-80 04:14a ▼ WPF14    .WPP   13,816  11-07-89 09:52p

1 Retrieve; 2 Delete; 3 Move/Rename; 4 Print; 5 Short/Long Display;
6 Look; 7 Other Directory; 8 Copy; 9 Find; N Name Search: 6
```

169

Figure 16-1. List Files screen

Otherwise, use the operating system date and time commands before using WordPerfect (see your operating system manual for information about these commands).

▶ *Directory*: This shows the directory for which documents are displayed.

▶ *Document size*: This identifies the size of the document currently highlighted.

▶ *Free and Used*: This shows the amount of space (in bytes, which are approximately one character) available (free) on your disk and the amount used. Never allow the free space to dwindle to less than 10% of the total space. If space becomes short, move documents to another disk or delete unneeded documents.

▶ *Files*: This identifies the number of documents displayed.

▶ *The directories* (such as <CURRENT>): The directory you are using appears along with other available directories. To display the files for another directory, highlight it and press Enter.

▶ *The files*: This listing shows each file name, extension, and size (in bytes), as well as the date and time last accessed.

The options you have for manipulating files appear on the bottom two lines of the screen. We covered Options 1 Retrieve, 6 Look, and 7 Other Directory in Chapter 7. The remaining options are for managing documents, and we'll cover them in this chapter.

Using the List Files Screen

The List Files screen is designed to allow you to work with one document or with several at a time. If you are working with one document, just highlight it and perform the desired operation. Sometimes, however, you may want to work with several documents. For example, you may want to copy several documents to a disk, or to delete more than one document, or to move a few documents at once. To work with multiple documents, highlight one of the documents and press the asterisk (using Shift and * on most keyboards). An asterisk appears before the file name. Continue to mark as many files as you want. Figure 16-2 shows three files marked with asterisks: BENLET.WPP, BENLET41.WPP, and BENLET45.WPP. The operation you perform will affect all files marked with an asterisk. To eliminate the asterisk from a file name, highlight the document name and press the asterisk again.

If the number of documents on the List Files screen fills more than one screen, use PgUp and PgDn to move from screenful to screenful.

To leave the List Files screen, press F1 Cancel or F7 Exit.

Copying Documents

You will often copy documents in order to create backup copies in case a document becomes damaged or lost. One way to copy a document is to save it under another name or to save it to another disk.

Another way to copy documents is to use the List Files screen. The benefits of this procedure are that you can copy a file on disk (instead of having to retrieve it to your screen) and you can copy more than one document in a single operation.

170

```
11-19-89  07:24p              Directory C:\WP51\DOC\*.WPP
Document size:      378    Free: 14,108,672 Used:      8,695    Marked:      3

.    Current   <Dir>                      ..    Parent    <Dir>
1-5      .WPP       884   01-01-80 12:11a  *BELET    .WPP     1,081   01-01-80 01:15a
BELET10E.WPP     1,533   10-29-89 10:05p   BELET111.WPP    2,660   11-12-89 10:05p
BELET112.WPP     2,660   11-12-89 10:05p  *BELET141.WPP    3,409   11-12-89 10:23p
BELET142.WPP     3,481   11-12-89 10:22p  *BELET145.WPP    4,205   11-12-89 10:40p
BELET15E.WPP     4,205   11-12-89 10:46p   BELET41 .WPP      519   10-22-89 09:00a
BELET42 .WPP       561   10-22-89 09:11a   BELET45 .WPP      568   10-22-89 01:20p
BELET53 .WPP       788   10-28-89 02:20p   BELET76 .WPP      967   10-22-89 09:33p
BELET84 .WPP       904   10-22-89 09:45p   BENLET  .WPP    2,062   01-01-80 01:12a
BENLET11.WPP       831   01-01-80 01:09a   FIG10-5 .WPP      970   01-01-80 01:09a
FIG143  .WPP       922   11-12-89 10:29p   FIG144  .WPP    3,416   11-12-89 10:33p
WPF1    .WPP    13,707   10-28-89 03:18p   WPF1-50 .WPP   13,706   10-28-89 03:04p
WPF1-AS .WPP    12,541   10-28-89 03:05p   WPF10   .WPP   10,049   10-29-89 10:02p
WPF10-50.WPP    10,049   10-29-89 10:02p   WPF10-AS.WPP    9,553   10-29-89 10:03p
WPF11   .WPP    14,922   01-01-80 07:09a   WPF11-50.WPP   14,922   01-01-80 07:09a
WPF11-AS.WPP    13,659   01-01-80 07:10a   WPF12   .WPP   11,767   01-01-80 01:45p
WPF12-50.WPP    11,767   01-01-80 01:45p   WPF12-AS.WPP   10,566   01-01-80 01:46p
WPF13   .WPP    13,206   01-01-80 04:13a   WPF13-50.WPP   13,206   01-01-80 04:13a
WPF13-AS.WPP    11,973   01-01-80 04:14a   WPF14   .WPP   13,816   11-07-89 09:52p

1 Retrieve; 2 Delete; 3 Move/Rename; 4 Print; 5 Short/Long Display;
6 Look; 7 Other Directory; 8 Copy; 9 Find; N Name Search: 6
```

Figure 16-2. Three documents marked for work

To copy one or more document with the List Files screen, press F5 List Files or select List Files from the File menu. Enter the drive, directory, and document information and press Enter. To copy more than one document, mark each with an asterisk. To copy just one document, highlight it. Select 8 Copy. The following prompt appears depending on the number of files to copy:

(If one file)   Copy this file to
(If multiple files)   Copy marked files? No (Yes)
                       Copy all marked files to:

Enter the drive and path of the location to which to copy the files. Press Enter. If the file already exists on the disk, a message like this appears:

Replace A:\BENLET.WPP No (Yes)

Select Yes to copy over the file. The "copy from" version replaces the "copy to" version.

Q Copy One or More Document Files

1. Press F5 List Files or select List Files from the File menu.	The current directory is displayed.
2. Change the drive, path, and file information if desired and press Enter.	The List Files screen appears.
3. If you want to copy more than one file, mark each with an asterisk. To copy just one file, highlight it. Select *8* Copy.	Copy messages appear.
4. Enter the drive and path of the disk to which to copy the file, and press Enter.	A replace message appears for your response if the file is already on the disk; the files are copied. □

172

Deleting Documents

You may want to delete documents. Deleting a document is useful when you are sure you will not want that version of the document again. For example, let's say you've created a couple of different versions of BENLET.WPP for internal review. When one version is selected, you'll want to delete the other versions. This not only saves space but saves possible future confusion about which version was used.

> ⊘ **Caution:** When deleting, always proceed carefully. Check and double check the file you want to delete to make sure you will never again want the document. Once a document is deleted, it cannot be recovered.

To delete a document, press F5 List Files or select List Files from the File menu. Enter the drive, directory, and file information then press Enter. If you want to delete multiple documents, mark each with an asterisk. Otherwise, just highlight the single document to delete. Then, select *2* Delete.

If you are deleting one file, a prompt like the following appears:

Delete: C:\WP51\DOC\BENLET.WPP No (Yes)

Make sure this is the document you want to delete. Select Yes to delete the file.

If you are deleting multiple files, each marked with an asterisk, a message like this appears:

Delete marked files? No (Yes)

Select Yes. This type of message appears:

Marked files will be deleted. Continue? No (Yes)

This is your chance to verify that you really *do* want to delete all the files marked with an asterisk. Select Yes again to delete these files.

173

 Delete One or More Document Files

1. Press F5 List Files or select List Files from the File menu.

   The current directory is displayed.

2. Change the drive, path, and file information, if desired, and press Enter.

   The List Files screen appears.

3. To delete multiple files, mark each with an asterisk or just highlight a file to delete. Select *2* Delete.

   Respond to the delete prompts as they appear.

Moving or Renaming Documents

You may move or rename documents through the List Files screen. As you'll see, though these features are handled through the same selection, the results are very different.

When you rename a file, the existing name is replaced with the new name you suggest. Renaming a file is useful when you determine a better way to organize existing files. For example, you may have created these three versions of a document:

DEARPT.WPP
DREPORT.WPP
DRT.WPP

You could rename these files to suggest the order in which they were created:

DERPT1.WPP
DERPT2.WPP
DERPT3.WPP

174

When you move a file, it is removed from the current disk location and placed at a new location you have indicated. For example, you might move a file from one disk to another when the original disk is getting full or if you want to store the file on a disk you use less often. Don't confuse moving a file with copying a file. When you move, the original location of the file is lost. When you copy, the original location of the file is preserved and a duplicate of the file is made.

To rename or move a file, press F5 List Files or select List Files from the File menu. Change the drive, path, and file information, if necessary, and press Enter. To move one or more files, mark the file(s) with an asterisk. To rename a file, just highlight the file you want to rename.

▶ **Hint:** You can only rename files one at a time. You can only move files by marking them with an asterisk.

Press *3* Move/Rename. If you are renaming a document, you will be prompted to enter the new name. If you are moving document(s), you will be prompted to enter the new drive and path location for the document(s). Respond to the appropriate prompts and the file(s) will be renamed or moved.

 Move or Rename Documents

1. Press F5 List Files or select List Files from the File menu.	The drive, path, and file information appears.

2. Enter new drive, path, and file information, if necessary. Press Enter.

The List Files screen appears.

3. Highlight the single file to rename or mark the file(s) to move with asterisk(s). Select *3* Move/Rename.

The prompts to rename or move the file(s) appear.

4. Follow the prompts.

The highlighted file is renamed or the files marked with asterisks are moved.

Saving and Using Documents in Other Formats

If you exchange work with other users of WordPerfect or personal computers, you may need to put your document file in another format or convert a different format to WordPerfect. WordPerfect can do.

WordPerfect to WordPerfect

Suppose you are exchanging files with people using an earlier version of WordPerfect. You can use their files since WordPerfect automatically converts earlier versions to the latest and greatest version. If any codes do not readily convert, WordPerfect inserts messages in your text to alert you to possible code conflicts you will need to resolve.

If you want to do the reverse (have the document that you created with the latest WordPerfect version used by someone with an earlier version) you need to convert the file to the exact earlier version. (Find out the version number from the person who will be using the document file.)

To convert to an earlier WordPerfect version, retrieve the document to convert. Press Ctrl-F5 Text In/Out and then *3* Save As or select Text Out from the File menu. These options (among others) appear:

```
WordPerfect 5.0
WordPerfect 4.2
```

Choose the version of WordPerfect you want. A message like the following gives you the opportunity to name the document:

```
Document to be saved (WP 5.0):
```

> ▶ **Hint:** Give the document a different name from its current name. Some users like naming schemes that suggest the version, such as MYDOC51.WPP for the 5.1 version and MYDOC50.WPP or MYDOC.W50 for a 5.0 version.

176   Type in the name and press Enter. The file is saved in the WordPerfect version you've selected.

Generic Files and DOS Text

You may need to exchange a document file with someone who is not using WordPerfect. Or you may want to send your document over the phone lines (via a device called a modem). In either case, you may save your document in a file format more appropriate to the job than the typical WordPerfect format.

These are the two file formats from which you may choose:

▶ *Generic*: A file saved in this format is saved without WordPerfect codes. The text is left in place and spaces replace the codes for formats like tabs and centering.

▶ *DOS Text*: The file is saved without the codes. Only the text, spaces, and hard returns (where you pressed Enter) remain. This file format is sometimes called an ASCII file (pronounced AS'-KEE).

To save the document on your screen in the generic file format, press Ctrl-F5 Text In/Out and select *3* Save As or select Text Out from the File menu. Select the Generic option. In response to the prompt, give the file a name (different from the current document name in order to preserve the WordPerfect version). Press Enter and the document is saved in the Generic file format.

To save the document on your screen in the DOS text format, press Ctrl-F5 Text In/Out and select *1* DOS Text then *1* Save or select Text Out then DOS Text from the File menu. Enter a new name for the document at the prompt and press Enter. The DOS text file is saved.

You may also convert a DOS text file for use with Word-Perfect. When you do this, two options (both a little confusing at first glance) are presented:

> *1 CR/LF to [HRt]*: When you use this option, carriage returns at the ends of lines will be converted to hard returns. Text will not "wrap around."
>
> *2 CR/LF to [SRt] in HZone*: If you select this option, carriage returns at the ends of lines will be converted to soft returns. This is more like the typical WordPerfect format in which you edit text and it wraps around to new margins. (HZone stands for hyphenation zone, which identifies where the soft return will be placed.)

Figure 16-3 shows a document retrieved with the CR/LF to [HRt] option. In this figure you can see that a hard return [HRt] has been inserted at the end of each line. To use this file effectively with WordPerfect's editing features, you would have to delete many of these hard returns. WordPerfect would then put soft returns in the appropriate spots.

Figure 16-4 illustrates the same document retrieved with CR/LF to [SRt]. Notice that soft returns are appropriately entered in the paragraph beginning "Your friend, Jim Miller." There are hard returns in the paragraph beginning "Barbara has consistently." This is because the paragraph is indented from the right margin and much of the paragraph does not fall in WordPerfect's hyphenation zone. This example illustrates that you must check text that is indented from the right margin and edit any misplaced hard returns.

To convert a DOS text file to WordPerfect, start with a "clear" screen. If you will convert using hard returns, make the margins less than those in the document (zero right and left margins are good). Because hard returns are entered, lines tend to be a little longer and may inappropriately wrap around with regular margin settings. If you will convert using soft returns,

177

178

```
File Edit Search Layout Mark Tools Font Graphics Help
─────────────────────────────────────────────────────────
plauded my work on our exposition with these
remarks at the dinner presentation:

     "Barbara has consistently proven
     that she goes above and beyond our
     expectations.  And... always within
     budget no less!"

     I look forward to speaking with you
C:\WP51\DOC\BENLET.ASC                    Doc 1 Pg 1 Ln 5.17" Pos 1"
[  ▲    ▲    ▲    ▲    ▲    ▲    ▲    ▲    ▲    ▲    ▲    ▲
-       Certificates of achievement[HRt]
[HRt]
     Your friend, Jim Miller, recently ap-[HRt]
plauded my work on our exposition with these[HRt]
remarks at the dinner presentation:[HRt]
[HRt]
     "Barbara has consistently proven[HRt]
     that she goes above and beyond our[HRt]
     expectations.  And... always within[HRt]
     budget no less!"[HRt]

Press Reveal Codes to restore screen
```

Figure 16-3. Carriage return/line feed converted to hard returns

```
File Edit Search Layout Mark Tools Font Graphics Help
─────────────────────────────────────────────────────────
          plauded my work on our exposition with these
          remarks at the dinner presentation:

               "Barbara has consistently proven
               that she goes above and beyond our
               expectations.  And... always within
               budget no less!"

               I look forward to speaking with you
C:\WP51\DOC\BENLET.ASC                    Doc 1 Pg 1 Ln 5.33" Pos 2"
   ▲   {   ▲    ▲    ▲    ▲    ▲    ▲    ▲    }   ▲    ▲    ▲
[-]       Certificates of achievement[HRt]
[HRt]
     Your friend, Jim Miller, recently ap[-]
plauded my work on our exposition with these[SRt]
remarks at the dinner presentation:[HRt]
[HRt]
     "Barbara has consistently proven[HRt]
     that she goes above and beyond our[HRt]
     expectations.  And... always within[SRt]
     budget no less!"[HRt]

Press Reveal Codes to restore screen
```

Figure 16-4. Carriage return/line feed converted to soft returns

enter the margins that are in the document if they are different from WordPerfect's default of 1 inch each. (Remember, set margins via Shift-F8 Format then *1* Line or by selecting Line from the Layout menu.)

Once you've entered the margins, press Ctrl-F5 Text In/Out and *1* DOS Text or select Text In from the File menu. Identify whether you want CR/LF to [HRt] or CR/LF to [SRt]. At the prompt, enter the name of the document to be retrieved and press Enter. The text is retrieved into a WordPerfect file. When you save the document, remember to give it an appropriate name.

Summary

179

In this chapter you've learned:

▶ To manipulate multiple documents on the list files screen, mark the documents with an asterisk. Press the asterisk again on the highlighted name to remove the mark.

▶ Usually, to manipulate only one document from the list files screen, highlight that document only.

▶ To copy, delete, or move one or more documents, press F5 List Files or select List Files from the File menu. Identify the document(s) with asterisks. Select the option desired and follow the prompts.

▶ To rename a document, highlight the document and then press F5 List Files or select List Files from the Files menu. Highlight the document. Select Rename and respond to each prompt.

▶ To save a document into another format, press Ctrl-F5 Text In/Out and select 1 DOS Text or 3 Save As, followed by the WordPerfect format. Or, select Text Out from the File menu and identify the format. Follow the prompts.

▶ To retrieve a DOS text file into WordPerfect, press Ctrl-F5 Text In/Out and select 1 DOS Text or select Text Out and DOS Text from the File menu. Identify the DOS text option and continue according to the prompts.

Chapter 17

Search for and Replace (Almost) Anything

In This Chapter

▶ *How to search forward*
▶ *How to search backward*
▶ *How to replace*

Uses of Search and Replace

You use WordPerfect's Search feature to find text and codes in a document. You type in the text or codes to search for and Word-Perfect finds the first occurrence. If you wish, you can then continue searching from that location.

There are more uses for Search than may meet the eye. You can search for text that you believe may be incorrectly entered. Or you can search for a key word in order to find a particular spot in a document. Search is also useful for checking headings, figure numbering, or bulleted text against tables of contents or indexes. You can also quickly scan a document page by page by searching for nonsense text that is not included in the document.

Figure 17-1 illustrates one use of Search. Here, the document will be checked for Bennington being misspelled as Benningtin. Notice that the last line of the screen shows the text that is sought. Figure 17-2 shows that the spelling is not found (notice the * Not Found * message at the bottom of the screen). You know that in this document, at least, Bennington is not Benningtin.

```
 File Edit Search Layout Mark Tools Font Graphics Help
 ───────────────────────────────────────────────────────
                        Barbara J. Wiley
                        3421 Pecos Way
                  San Diego, California 92123

        Mr. David Randolph
        Bennington Corporation
        45 Superstition Highway
        Phoenix, Arizona 85252

                                        May 12, 1991


        Dear Mr. Randolph:

                As I discussed, I am very interested in
        pursuing a career with the Bennington
        Corporation.  I have attached:

        -       My resume with a chronological work histo-
                ry as requested
        -       Letters of recommendation
 -> Srch: Benningtin
```

Figure 17-1. Checking for Benningtin

The Replace feature goes a step beyond searching. With it, you identify both the text to find *and* the text to replace the found text. Replace is useful if you realize a proper name is misspelled consistently, a code is incorrectly used, or you wish to change formatting. For example, for a bulleted list, you might have entered text with a small "o" (to signify a bullet) followed by a Tab. In order to change that to a dash followed by an indent, you could use Replace.

Let's take a look at an example. In our letter, bullets are created by a dash followed by an indent. We'll replace those

```
File Edit Search Layout Mark Tools Font Graphics Help
                      Barbara J. Wiley
                       3421 Pecos Way
                 San Diego, California 92123


     Mr. David Randolph
     Bennington Corporation
     45 Superstition Highway
     Phoenix, Arizona 85252

                                    May 12, 1991


     Dear Mr. Randolph:

          As I discussed, I am very interested in
     pursuing a career with the Bennington
     Corporation.  I have attached:

     -    My resume with a chronological work histo-
          ry as requested
     -    Letters of recommendation
   * Not found *
```

183

Figure 17-2. Benningtin not found

with an indent, a small o, and an indent. Figure 17-3 shows at the bottom of the screen the text that will be searched. We include the indent after the dash because we only want to find occurrences where the dash is followed by an indent (not dashes that might be hyphens, for example). Figure 17-4 shows the text we want to use in replacement. Finally, Figure 17-5 illustrates the text after the replacement is made. Notice that the indents and small o's are now included.

You can check your replacements as you work or let WordPerfect do it alone. If you check replacements, WordPerfect stops at each occurrence. You then identify whether to replace that occurrence or not.

When you search and replace, the text you type in is important to identifying what will be found and, potentially, replaced. Here are the rules to keep in mind:

▶ When you enter the text to search out in lowercase letters, both lower- and uppercase letters will be found. (For example, entering "merger" will find "merger," "Merger," and "MERGER.") If you enter uppercase

```
File Edit Search Layout Mark Tools Font Graphics Help

Dear Mr. Randolph:

        As I discussed, I am very interested in
pursuing a career with the Bennington
Corporation.  I have attached:

   -    My resume with a chronological work histo-
        ry as requested
   -    Letters of recommendation
   -    Certificates of achievement

        Your friend, Jim Miller, recently ap-
plauded my work on our exposition with these
remarks at the dinner presentation:

        "Barbara has consistently proven
        that she goes above and beyond our
        expectations.  And... always within
        budget no less!"

        I look forward to speaking with you
further on June 8th.  I'll meet you at your
-> Srch: [-][→Indent]
```

184

Figure 17-3. The dash and indent entered for the search

```
File Edit Search Layout Mark Tools Font Graphics Help

Dear Mr. Randolph:

        As I discussed, I am very interested in
pursuing a career with the Bennington
Corporation.  I have attached:

   -    My resume with a chronological work histo-
        ry as requested
   -    Letters of recommendation
   -    Certificates of achievement

        Your friend, Jim Miller, recently ap-
plauded my work on our exposition with these
remarks at the dinner presentation:

        "Barbara has consistently proven
        that she goes above and beyond our
        expectations.  And... always within
        budget no less!"

        I look forward to speaking with you
further on June 8th.  I'll meet you at your
Replace with: [→Indent]o[→Indent]
```

Figure 17-4. The indent, small o, and indent to replace

```
File Edit Search Layout Mark Tools Font Graphics Help
───────────────────────────────────────────────────────────

    Dear Mr. Randolph:

        As I discussed, I am very interested in
    pursuing a career with the Bennington
    Corporation.  I have attached:

            o       My resume with a chronological work
                    history as requested
            o       Letters of recommendation
            o       Certificates of achievement

        Your friend, Jim Miller, recently ap-
    plauded my work on our exposition with these
    remarks at the dinner presentation:

            "Barbara has consistently proven
            that she goes above and beyond our
            expectations.  And... always within
            budget no less!"

        I look forward to speaking with you
C:\WP51\DOC\BELET15E.WPP                    Doc 1 Pg 1 Ln 4.67" Pos 2.5"
```

185

Figure 17-5. After replacements

letters, however, only matches with the same capital
letters will be found. (If you enter "Merger," "Merger"
will be identified but not "merger" or "MERGER.")

▶ When text is replaced, the case used in the replacement
will match the replaced text. (For example, if "Merger"
is encountered and you are replacing with the word
"consolidation," the replacement is entered with the
first letter capitalized just like the text being replaced.)

▶ To search for a code, press the keys you would press for
the function. (You must use the key presses not the
menu choices.) For example, to search for the [BOLD]
code, press F6 Bold. *Do not* type in [BOLD] using
brackets and capital letters.

▶ Pay attention to your use of spaces and hard returns
when you search. If you enter spaces or press Enter, the
spaces or hard return will be included in the search. If
you leave out spaces or hard returns, words that include
the searched-out text will be found. For example, if you
enter the letters "creat" without spaces before and after,
words like "recreate," "create," "recreation," and

"creative" will be found. If you enter "create" with a space before and after the letters, only the word "create" will be found.

▶ If no occurrence of the text is found, this message appears:

`* Not found *`

▶ If you think there is text to be found, repeat the operation. Check the text entered to be searched for to make sure it is correct.

Searching Forward

186

Searching forward in a document means searching from your cursor location to the end of the document. If you want to search the entire document, press Home, Home, Home, Up Arrow to move to the top of the document (before any codes). Then, to start searching forward, press F2 Search or select Forward on the Search menu. This prompt appears.

`-> Srch:`

Enter the text and/or codes for which you are searching.

 Hint: *Do not* press Enter unless you want to search for hard returns.

Once the text is entered, press F2 Search. The first occurrence of the searched-for text is marked by your cursor. To search out the next occurrence, press the search keystrokes again.

 Search Forward

1. Position your cursor where the search should begin. Press F2 Search or select Forward from the Search menu.

This prompt appears:
`-> Srch:`

2. Enter the text and/or codes   The text is found.
   to search and press F2
   Search.   □

> ▶ **Hint:** When you search, only the document text is
> searched. If you have created headers, footers, foot-
> notes, endnotes, or graphic boxes and want to search the
> text in them as well, press Home before using the F2
> Search option. Or select Extended from the Search menu,
> then search Forward. This prompt appears:
> Extended srch:

Searching Backward   187

To search from your cursor position back to the beginning of the
document is referred to as searching backward. To search from
the end of the document to the beginning, press Home, Home,
Home, Down Arrow to go the end of the document (after all
codes).
    To search backward, press Shift-F2 Search Backward or
select Backward from the Search menu. This prompt appears:

<-Srch:

Notice that the arrow in the prompt points backward. Type in
the text and/or codes to search out. Press F2 Search to start the
search function. The first occurrence of the searched-out text is
found. To continue the search, just repeat the keystrokes.

 Search Backward

1. Position your cursor where   This prompt appears:
   the search should begin.   <-Srch:
   Press Shift-F2 Search
   Backward or select
   Backward from the Search
   menu.

2. Enter the text and/or codes to search and press F2 Search.

The text is found.

> ▶ **Hint:** When you search, only the document text is searched. To search headers, footers, footnotes, endnotes, or graphic boxes you've created, press Home before using the Shift-F2 Search Backward option. Or select Extended from the Search screen and then Search Backward.

188   Replacing Text

To replace text, place your cursor where you want the new text located. Text from the cursor to the end of the document will be searched out and replaced. Press Alt-F2 Replace or select Replace from the Search menu. This prompt (standing for "with confirm") appears:

w/Confirm? No (Yes)

If you want to confirm each replacement, type *y*. If you want WordPerfect to automatically replace each occurrence, type *n*. Until you are accustomed to replacing text, it is a good idea to confirm replacements. That way, you can see exactly what WordPerfect is replacing and be assured that that is what you intended.

Once you have identified whether to confirm replacements or not, this prompt appears to indicate that you will search forward from your cursor location:

-> Srch:

Type in the text and/or codes to search out and press F2 Search. This prompt appears:

Replace with:

Enter the text to be used as replacement text and press F2 Search again.

If you do not want to confirm each replacement, all replacements are automatically made. If you opted to confirm replacements, you are taken to the first occurrence. This prompt appears:

`Confirm? No (Yes)`

Type *y* if you want to replace the occurrence marked by your cursor. Type *n* if you want to go to the next occurrence. The process continues for the remainder of the document.

Q **Replacing Text**

1. Position your cursor where the Replace procedure should begin. Press Alt-F2 Replace or select Replace from the Search menu.

   This prompt appears:
   `w/Confirm? No (Yes)`

2. Respond *y* or *n* depending on whether you want to confirm each replacement.

   This prompt appears:
   `-> Srch:`

3. Enter the text and/or codes to search out and press F2 Search.

   The prompt appears:
   `Replace with:`

4. Enter the text and/or codes to replace and press F2 Search.

   If you will confirm replacements, you are taken to the first one to respond Yes or No. Otherwise, all replacements are automatically made. □

189

▶ **Hint:** Only the text in the document is searched and replaced. To look and replace in headers, footers, footnotes, endnotes, or graphic boxes, press Home before using the Alt-F2 Replace option. Or select Extended from the Search screen and then select Replace.

Summary

In this chapter you've learned:

- ▶ There are rules for searching and/or replacing upper- and lowercase letters, spaces, and codes.
- ▶ Searches and replaces occur from the location of the cursor forward or backward (as indicated by the prompt arrow).
- ▶ To search forward, press F2 Search or select Forward from the Search menu. Follow the prompts.
- ▶ To search backward, press Shift-F2 Search or select Backward from the Search menu. Follow the prompts.
- ▶ To replace text and/or codes, press Alt-F2 Replace or select Replace from the Search menu. Follow the prompts.
- ▶ To extend a search to include headers, footers, endnotes, footnotes, and graphics, press Home before making the Search or Replace keypress or select Extended from the Search menu and then select the operation you want.

Chapter 18

Working with Two Documents

In This Chapter

▶ *Why use two documents?*

▶ *How to use windows to view two documents at once*

▶ *How to use the Switch option to view two documents full-screen*

Why Use Two Documents?

Using two documents at a time has a variety of applications. The most significant is WordPerfect's ability to copy or move between documents. Say, for instance, you want to copy the return address from a letter to a new document to start a new letter. Figure 18-1 shows both documents on the screen at once. The screen is split to allow display of each document. The top of the screen contains the existing letter. The bottom of the screen is a "blank" document ready to be copied to. Figure 18-2 illustrates the result after the copy. The return address has been copied to the new document.

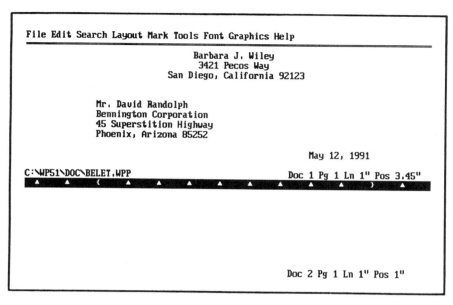

Figure 18-1. Existing letter and blank document before the copy

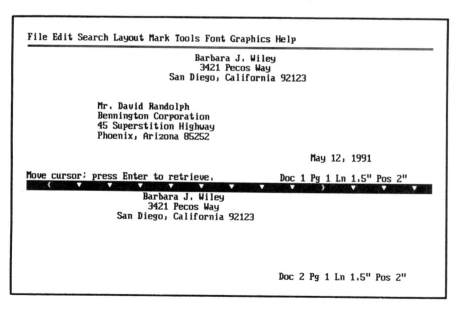

Figure 18-2. Existing letter and new document after the copy

You can also move text in the same way. For example, say you decide to move the resume information from the document called BELET.WPP into a document you'll call RESUME.WPP. Figure 18-3 shows the beginning of the resume information in BELET.WPP (in document 1). Notice that the lower right corner of the status line indicates "Doc 1." After blocking the appropriate text and then moving it, the text is placed in another full-screen document—document 2. Notice that in Figure 18-4 "Doc 2" appears in the lower right corner. The document has been saved as RESUME.WPP.

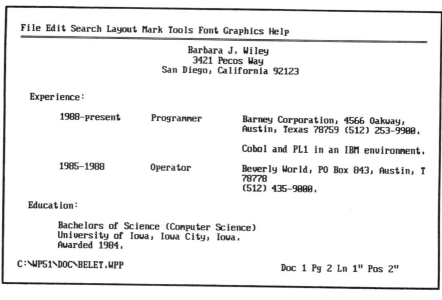

193

Figure 18-3. BELET.WPP contents in document 1

In addition to copying and moving text between documents, using two documents is useful if you wish to compare the contents of one document to another, or to look up references in a second document, or actually to build two documents at once. For example, you may have a stack of research that you need for two documents. By setting up two documents at once, you can scan the research and build both documents as you go.

```
File Edit Search Layout Mark Tools Font Graphics Help
─────────────────────────────────────────────────────────
                     Barbara J. Wiley
                      3421 Pecos Way
                San Diego, California 92123


Experience:

    1988-present      Programmer       Barney Corporation, 4566 Oakway,
                                       Austin, Texas 78759 (512) 253-9900.

                                       Cobol and PL1 in an IBM environment.

    1985-1988         Operator         Beverly World, PO Box 843, Austin, Tex
                                       78778
                                       (512) 435-9000.


Education:

    Bachelors of Science (Computer Science)
    University of Iowa, Iowa City, Iowa.
    Awarded 1984.

C:\WP51\DOC\RESUME.WPP                        Doc 2 Pg 1 Ln 1" Pos 3.49"
```

Figure 18-4. RESUME.WPP created by moving
BELET.WPP contents to document 2

There are two ways to display more than one document on the screen. The first is by using *windows*. Just like a window on a wall splits the wall into segments, windows on a computer screen create small screen portions. You can view documents through these windows. The second way to view two documents at once is through WordPerfect's *Switch* feature. With it, you switch from one full screen display to another with a special keypress.

Whether you use windows or switch between full-screen displays is really a matter of preference. Use which one is more comfortable for you. You have full WordPerfect editing capabilities with either option.

▶ **Hint:** WordPerfect only allows you to use two documents at once. You cannot open more than two windows or switch to a third document.

Windows

To split your screen into two windows, press Ctrl-F3 Screen. Type *1* Window. Or select Window from the Edit menu. This prompt appears:

Number of lines in this window:

Type in a number representing the number of lines for the current window (the window that will display the document currently on your screen). Most computer screens are 24 lines long. Entering 11 or 12 will cause the split to be roughly at the halfway point. Instead of entering the number, you can also move the up arrow or the down arrow to position the bar that separates the windows. After entering a number or positioning the bar, press Enter. Figure 18-5 illustrates the bar at the starting position. Figure 18-6 shows the result of pressing the up arrow five times from the starting position.

After you have identified the number of lines to be in the window, the screen splits. As shown in the earlier figures, the

195

```
File Edit Search Layout Mark Tools Font Graphics Help
─────────────────────────────────────────────────────────
                        Barbara J. Wiley
                         3421 Pecos Way
                   San Diego, California 92123


        Mr. David Randolph
        Bennington Corporation
        45 Superstition Highway
        Phoenix, Arizona 85252

                                        May 12, 1991


        Dear Mr. Randolph:

                As I discussed, I am very interested in
        pursuing a career with the Bennington
        Corporation.  I have attached:

                o       My resume with a chronological work
                        history as requested
Number of lines in this window: 21
    ▲    ▲    {    ▲    ▲    ▲    ▲    ▲    ▲    ▲    ▲    }    ▲
```

Figure 18-5. Window bar after selecting Window option

```
┌─────────────────────────────────────────────────────────────┐
│ File Edit Search Layout Mark Tools Font Graphics Help         │
│ ─────────────────────────────────────────────────────────── │
│                    Barbara J. Wiley                           │
│                    3421 Pecos Way                             │
│                San Diego, California 92123                    │
│                                                               │
│                                                               │
│         Mr. David Randolph                                    │
│         Bennington Corporation                                │
│         45 Superstition Highway                               │
│         Phoenix, Arizona 85252                                │
│                                                               │
│                                       May 12, 1991            │
│                                                               │
│             Dear Mr. Randolph:                                │
│ Number of lines in this window: 14                            │
│ ▄▄▄▄▄▄▄▄▄▄▄▄▄▄▄▄▄▄▄▄▄▄▄▄▄▄▄▄▄▄▄▄▄▄▄▄▄▄▄▄▄▄▄▄▄▄▄▄▄▄▄▄▄▄▄▄▄▄▄▄ │
│  ▲    ▲  (    ▲    ▲    ▲    ▲    ▲    ▲    ▲   }    ▲        │
│                    Barbara J. Wiley                           │
│                    3421 Pecos Way                             │
│                San Diego, California 92123                    │
│                                                               │
│                                                               │
│ Experience:                                                   │
│ C:\WP51\DOC\RESUME.WPP               Doc 2 Pg 1 Ln 1" Pos 3.49" │
└─────────────────────────────────────────────────────────────┘
```

Figure 18-6. Window bar after pressing up arrow five times

status-line information for each window appears at the bottom of that window. The arrows, left bracket, and right bracket in the bar illustrate the active window's tab settings, left margin, and right margin, respectively. To move from one window to the other, press Shift-F3 Switch. Or select Switch from the Edit menu.

To close a window, enter *24* for the number of lines (or the number of lines on your computer screen, if it is different). Or use the up or down arrow key to place the bar at the bottom of the screen.

▶ **Hint:** "Closing" a window in this manner just removes the display of one of the documents from the screen. If there is still text in the second document, you will be given a chance to save it before you leave Word-Perfect. To close a window completely, switch your cursor to that window, press F7 Exit or select Exit from the File menu, and proceed to dispose of the document in the window by choosing whether to save it.

Q Open, Switch, and Close a Window

1. To open a window, press Ctrl-F3 Screen and type *1* Window or select Window from the Edit menu.

   This message appears:
   `Number of lines in this window:`

2. Enter the number of lines and press Enter or move the up or down arrow and press Enter.

   The window is created.

3. To move between windows, press Shift-F3 Switch or select Switch from the Edit menu.

   The cursor moves to the other window. The bar reflects information for that window.

4. To close a window, repeat steps 1 and 2 and enter 24 for the lines or move the bar to the bottom of your screen.

   The display of the window disappears.

197

> ⊘ **Caution:** If you retrieve the same document into both windows and then edit one of the windows, the edits are not automatically applied to the document in the second window. If you make edits that you want to keep, make sure they are made in one document and then that you have that document saved under the appropriate name. The best policy when working with the same document in both windows is to be careful about which document is the "latest and greatest" to save.

To copy or move between documents, just switch to the new document after identifying the text to copy or move. Then complete the operation.

The Switch Option

Instead of displaying two windows on the screen at once, you can switch between full-screen displays of two documents. To switch to a new display, press Shift-F3 Switch or select Switch from the Edit menu. You are taken to the other full-screen display. "Doc 1" or "Doc 2" appears in the bottom right corner of the screen, enabling you to distinguish between the two documents. Continue to use Switch to move back and forth between the full-screen displays.

Q Switch to Second Full-Screen Display

1. To switch to a second full-screen document display, press Shift-F3 Switch or select Switch from the Edit menu.

   You are taken to the second document display.

2. Use Switch to move between document displays.

   Doc 1 or Doc 2 appears in the lower right corner of your screen. ☐

To copy or move between displays, identify the text to copy or move, switch to the new display, and complete the copy or move.

To complete activity on one document, use F7 Exit or select Exit from the File menu. Complete the Save option for that document. If you load the same document in both document displays, however, edits to one display will not "take" in the document in the other display. Make sure when you save that you save the correct document.

Summary

In this chapter you've learned:

▶ You can fully edit two documents at the same time (including copying and moving text between documents).

▶ To create a window, press Ctrl-F3 Screen and select 1 Window or select Window from the Edit menu. Enter the lines or move the arrow keys to identify the window length. Press Enter.

198

▶ To switch between full screen displays (or windows), press Shift-F3 Switch or select Switch from the Edit menu.

▶ To "close" a window, enter the number of lines as 24 (on most computers). To save and exit a window or document display, use F7 Exit (or Exit from the File menu) as usual.

199

The Professional Touch: Headers and Footers

In This Chapter

▶ *What are headers and footers?*
▶ *How to create and edit headers and footers*
▶ *How to discontinue a header or footer*

What Are Headers and Footers?

Headers and footers are common text that appear at the top (head) or the bottom (foot) of a page. Headers and footers can add a professional touch to a document to give it a first rate appearance. Let's consider some examples.

A header or footer may include the name of a document, version number, notification of status (draft or confidential, for instance), author's name, page number, chapter or section numbers, graphics, or any other appropriate text you care to include. For example, these are possible header or footer lines:

Chapter 3   page 3-16

CONFIDENTIAL from the President's office   page 6 of 9

Year End Report   - DRAFT -   by Jim Lindy
                                                  Please Turn the Page

(c)1990 Webber Corporation

    Don't let these examples fool you. A header or footer can be more than a single line; in fact, it can include up to one pageful of text. This allows you great flexibility in the amount of information you can place in a header or footer. When you create headers and footers, you can use all of WordPerfect's editing features.

    To place a page number in the header or footer, press Ctrl-B to get this symbol: ^B. Every time this symbol is encountered in a header or footer, WordPerfect will increment the page number by one. To start page numbering with a number other than 1, set the New Page Number to the desired first number. (Use Shift-F8 Format, 2 Page, 6 Page Numbering, and 1 New Page Number. See Chapter 13 to review this procedure.)

202

> ⊘ **Caution:** Do not use the Page Number Position feature (through Format, Page, and Page Numbering) when you are using headers with page numbers or you may wind up with two page numbers. One page number will be positioned through that feature and the other page number will be the one contained in the header.

    You place the header or footer in the document and a code appears in your document to mark the start of the header or footer. The header or footer is then automatically repeated on each page or on alternating pages, depending on your selection. Every time you enter a new header or footer code, that header or footer is used until you enter another code. As a result, you can enter a header for front matter, such as:

Design Forward

Then, after those pages, enter the chapters:

Chapter 1 of Design   page 1-1

Finally, enter a header for an appendix:

```
Design Appendix A                                          App A-1
```

Because you can change headers and footers as often as you like, all parts of this document can be placed in one document file.

> ▶ **Hint:** When printed, headers and footers are placed under and above the top and bottom margins, respectively. They are not considered part of the margin setting.

Creating Headers and Footers   203

To create a header, place your cursor at the top of the first page for the header (before all codes except Paper Size Type or Top/ Bottom Margin codes). To create a footer, place your cursor where on the page you want the footer to begin. It is a good practice to place both the header and footer codes at the top of the page. That way, you can find them easily.

After positioning the cursor, press Shift-F8 Format and select *2* Page. Or select Page from the Layout menu. The Format: Page menu appears. Select 3 Headers or 4 Footers depending on your desire. A line like this appears:

```
1 Header A; 2 Header B:
```

You can place two headers or footers on a page, which is useful if you have entered one header as Header A and then want to add more text to the header. Instead of editing it, you can add Header B. Get in the practice of always choosing Header A or Footer A first. Then, if a Header B or Footer B is necessary, you will know you are adding to the first header or footer on the page.

After selecting 1 for Header A or Footer A, you see a line like this:

```
1 Discontinue; 2 Every Page; 3 Odd Pages; 4 Even Pages; 5 Edit:
```

enabling you to place headers or footers on every page, just on odd numbered pages, or just on even numbered pages. For example, the text pages of this book have different headers for even and odd numbered pages. You will probably want the header on every page for most documents. Make the appropriate selection and you are taken to the header or footer screen. A sample of this screen is shown in Figure 19-1.

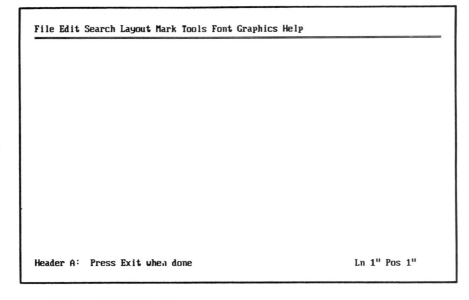

```
File Edit Search Layout Mark Tools Font Graphics Help




Header A:  Press Exit when done                    Ln 1" Pos 1"
```

Figure 19-1. Header screen

The header or footer screen is just like a regular WordPerfect screen. You can use any editing capability when you are entering the header or footer text. Once you've entered the text, press F7 Exit or select Exit from the File menu. Continue exiting until you return to your document screen. A code like this is placed in your document:

```
[Header A:Every page;Chapter 16[Flsh Rgt]Page 16[-]^B[HRt]
By: Jim Wilson... ]
```

Let's take a closer look at the code example just shown. It first identifies whether the text is a header or a footer. In this example, it is a header. Then, the code identifies whether it is Header or Footer A or B. Next, the frequency of the header or footer appears. This header will appear on every page. The beginning of the text and codes contained in the header are next shown. In the example, Chapter 16 is followed by a flush right code in order to place Page 16-^B at the right margin. The ^B is created by pressing Ctrl-B and it will be replaced with consecutive page numbering when the document is printed. A hard return follows and then the author's name. The elipses (...) indicate there is more text in the header than appears in the code. To see the complete header text, you would need to edit the header (which is described later in this chapter).

Let's look at an example of a header and footer using the resume for Barbara J. Wiley. In Figure 19-2, our RESUME.WPP document appears with headers and footers added. Notice in the Reveal Codes screen at the bottom that the code for Header A appears after the margin-setting code. The code for Footer A follows the code for Header A and both are set up to appear on every page. Figure 19-3 shows the header that was entered. Notice that the header consists of two vertical lines. Figure 19-4 illustrates the footer—a single vertical line. The font code for Times Roman is entered (be sure your printer handles the font you choose). The text "Resume of Barbara J. Wiley" follows. The flush right code places the current date in the right

205

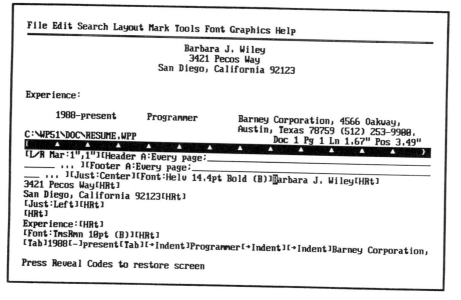

Figure 19-2. RESUME.WPP with header and footer codes

corner. The printed appearance of the first page of this resume is shown in Figure 19-5. This header and footer will be printed on each page.

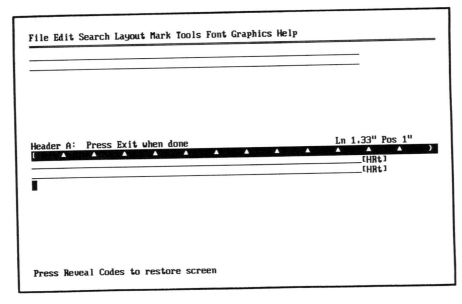

File Edit Search Layout Mark Tools Font Graphics Help

Header A: Press Exit when done   Ln 1.33" Pos 1"

Press Reveal Codes to restore screen

Figure 19-3. The header for the resume

Q Adding a Header or Footer

1. Place your cursor in the location for the header or footer. Press Shift-F8 Format and select *2* Page or select Page from the Layout menu.

    The Format: Page menu appears.

2. Select 3 Headers or 4 Footers.

    A prompt like this appears:
    1 Header A; 2 Header B:

3. Go with the A choice unless this is a second header or footer on the page.

    A prompt with new options appears.

4. Select the placement of the header or footer:

    You are taken to the header or footer screen.

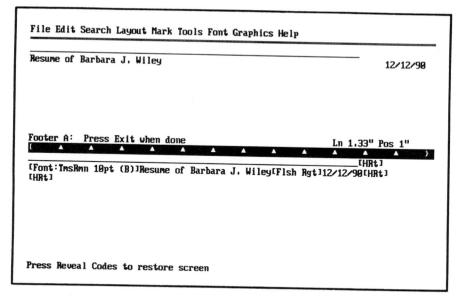

Figure 19-4. The footer for the resume

2 Every page
3 Odd pages
4 Even pages

5. Enter the header or footer text just like any WordPerfect text. When you are done, press F7 Exit or select Exit from the File menu. Continue exiting until you return to the document screen.

A code for the header of footer is placed in your document.

Editing Headers and Footers

To edit a header or footer, place your cursor on or after the code representing the header or footer you want to edit. Press Shift-F8 Format then *1* Page or select Page from the Layout menu. On the

208

Barbara J. Wiley
3421 Pecos Way
San Diego, California 92123

Experience:

1988-present	Programmer	Barney Corporation, 4566 Oakway, Austin, Texas 78759 (512) 253-9900.
		Cobol and PL1 in an IBM environment.
1985-1988	Operator	Beverly World, PO Box 843, Austin, Texas 78778 (512) 435-9000.

Education:

Bachelors of Science (Computer Science)
University of Iowa, Iowa City, Iowa.
Awarded 1984.

Affiliations:

Data Processing Professional Group. 1985 to present.

Resume of Barbara J. Wiley   12/12/90

Figure 19-5. The printed result of RESUME.WPP with header and footer

Format: Page menu select *3* Header or *4* Footer. Enter the number for Header or Footer A or B when it appears. This line appears:

```
1 Discontinue; 2 Every Page; 3 Odd Pages; 4 Even Pages; 5 Edit:
```

Press 5 for Edit and you are taken to the existing header or footer screen. Edit it as you would any WordPerfect document screen. When you're done, press F7 Exit or select Exit from the Layout menu. Continue exiting until you reach the document screen. The new, edited header or footer takes effect.

Discontinuing Headers or Footers

If you want to discontinue the use of a header or footer, put your cursor on or after the header or footer code. Press Shift-F8 Format then *1* Page or select Page from the Layout menu. From the Format: Page menu, select 3 Header or 4 Footer. Select Header A or B or Footer A or B. This line appears:

```
1 Discontinue; 2 Every Page; 3 Odd Pages; 4 Even Pages; 5 Edit:
```

209

Press *1* to discontinue the header or footer. Then press F7 Exit or select Exit from the Layout menu. Continue exiting until you reach the document screen. A code like this is placed in your text:

```
[Header B:Discontinue]
```

Summary

In this chapter you've learned:

► A header is text that appears at the top of the document page (after the top margin). A footer appears at the bottom of the page (before the bottom margin).

► To add a header or footer, press Shift-F8 Format and select 2 Page or select Page from the Layout menu. Continue following the prompts and complete the header or footer screen. Press F7 Exit or select Exit from the File menu when the header or footer text is entered.

► To edit or to discontinue a header or footer, press Shift-F8 and select 2 Page or select Page from the Layout menu. Continue to follow the prompts and select Discontinue or Edit as desired.

Chapter 20

Automating with Macros

In This Chapter

▶ *Why and when to use macros*
▶ *How to automatically replay keystrokes with a macro*
▶ *How to edit a macro*

Macros: Why and When

In this chapter you will learn how to automate your activities to save time and effort. Okay, you thought the computer alone is automation enough? With an investment of just a little time, you can discover a slick way to make WordPerfect automatically perform tasks specific to your own needs.

A *macro* is a special file you can create with WordPerfect to store your keystrokes and commands. Anytime you want to replay the contents of the macro, just call it up and the rest is automatic.

When might you use a macro? There are plenty of opportunities. You may want to create a macro to automatically type in your return address, your name, or other names and addresses you commonly use. Or you may want to use a macro to store formatting codes you commonly use. For example, if you often create letters with 1.5-inch margins and with justification off, you can enter those commands once in a macro and then replay them in any document.

Another good use of macros is to store your common headers or footers. You can enter all the keystrokes, from creating the header or footer through exiting the header or footer screen, in a macro. Placing header or footer activities in a macro saves both in conserved keystrokes and in the effort of recalling exactly how you set up the header or footer last time (maybe even having to look in an old document).

How do you know what macros to create? That's easy. Just watch what you do. Especially pay attention to those activities you perform over and over, those that seem tedious, and those that could be faster or more pleasant if you let WordPerfect do them for you. Since virtually any WordPerfect keystrokes can be in a macro, your limit is your imagination and your mastery of the steps to create and use macros.

Defining a Macro

The easy way to get started using macros is to create one by entering keystrokes and recording them as you go. Creating a macro in this way is referred to as "defining" the macro. Let's look at an example. Suppose Barbara Wiley often uses her return address centered on the page (as in the letter shown in Figure 20-1). A macro is a good way to store and replay this type of text.

To create the macro, press Ctrl-F10 Macro Define or select Macro and then Define from the Tools menu. This prompt appears in the bottom left corner of the screen:

`Define macro:`

You would now name the macro. You enter this name when you want to use the macro. There are two options for naming it. Use the approach with which you feel most comfortable.

```
File Edit Search Layout Mark Tools Font Graphics Help
                        Barbara J. Wiley
                         3421 Pecos Way
                   San Diego, California 92123

    Mr. David Randolph
    Bennington Corporation
    45 Superstition Highway
    Phoenix, Arizona 85252

                                   May 12, 1991

    Dear Mr. Randolph:

         As I discussed, I am very interested in
    pursuing a career with the Bennington
    Corporation.  I have attached:

         o    My resume with a chronological work
              history as requested
         o    Letters of recommendation
    C:\WP51\DOC\BELET.WPP              Doc 1 Pg 1 Ln 1" Pos 3.45"
```

Figure 20-1. Return address centered

213

1. Type in eight or fewer letters. (You don't include an extension with macros. WordPerfect automatically adds .WPM to the end, for "WordPerfect Macro.") Press Enter. Using this naming approach allows you to enter a descriptive name. Our example might be called BRETADD for "Barbara's RETurn ADDress."

2. Hold down the Alt key and type in any letter. The benefit of this naming approach is that you only have to make two keypresses when you later use the macro. For example, you could press down Alt and enter B (for Barbara's return address). The problem with this approach is that you could end up with a lot of macros you can't identify later. Or you could wind up wanting to use the same Alt-letter combination for another macro.

If you accidentally enter a macro name that you've already used, a prompt like this one appears:

BRETADD.WPM Already Exists: 1 Replace; 2 Edit; 3 Description:

To quit defining the macro and begin again with a different name, just press F1 Cancel. If you want to completely replace the macro keystrokes with different keystrokes, press *1* Replace. (Options 2 and 3 are covered in "Editing a Macro" later in this chapter.) Selecting 1 Replace, gives you a "second chance" message like this:

`Replace C:\WP51\BRETADD.WPM? No (Yes)`

Type *n* to return to your document or *y* to totally replace the contents of the macro.

After entering the name for the macro you are defining, this prompt appears:

`Description:`

This is an opportunity to enter a brief description of the macro. Include information about the contents of the macro or its use. For example, we might use

214

`Description:` Barbara's RETurn ADDress, Centered

to identify not only what the letters in the macro name stand for but also the fact that the return address is centered. Once you've typed in the description, press Enter.

This prompt blinks at the bottom left of the screen to remind you that any keystrokes you enter will be placed in the macro:

`Macro Def`

Type in the text and WordPerfect key combinations. You can use most WordPerfect editing capabilities. (You cannot use a mouse, however, to position the cursor within a macro.)

As you enter the keystrokes, you may make a typographical error or mistakenly press an incorrect command. If you make a mistake that you can correct, first finish the macro keystrokes. Then you can either use the macro with the mistake and its correction (if no harm is done) or you can edit the macro contents (covered later in this chapter). As an example of the former, say you typed in this text when entering a macro:

`San Dieb`

To correct, you'd press the backspace key to get to

`San Die`

Then you'd complete the correct keystrokes before continuing:

`San Diego`

When the macro is later replayed, the "b," backspace, and "g" would all be replayed. It happens very fast though, and you could decide not to edit it.

Once the macro text is entered, just press Ctrl-F10 Macro Define or select Macro and Define from the Tools menu. The blinking message

`Macro Def`

goes away to signify that the macro is complete and you are back to regular WordPerfect editing.

215

Q Defining a Macro

1. Press Ctrl-F10 Macro Define or select Macro, then Define from the Tools menu.

   This messages appears:
   `Define macro:`

2. Type in an eight-character (or less) name and press Enter or press Alt and a letter.

   This message appears:
   `Description:`

3. Type in a brief description and press Enter.

   `Macro Def` blinks on the lower corner of the screen.

4. Enter the keystrokes for the macro. When done, press Ctrl-F10 Macro Define or select Macro, then Define from the Tools menu.

   `Macro Def` disappears. The macro is defined.

A good way to display the names of available macros is to press F5 List Files or select List Files from the File menu. At the Dir: directory listing, type in *.WPM* as the file extension in order to display only macros files. For example:

`Dir: C:\WP51\*.WPM`

A screen like that in Figure 20-2, displaying only macro files, would appear.

```
12-04-89  09:23p                Directory C:\WP51\*.WPM
Document size:    2,127  Free:      903,168 Used:         304     Files:        2

    .   Current     <Dir>                 |  ..    Parent    <Dir>
  BRETADD .WPM        231  12-04-89 09:19p |  TOCM     .WPM        73  10-02-89 08:34p




1 Retrieve; 2 Delete; 3 Move/Rename; 4 Print; 5 Short/Long Display;
6 Look; 7 Other Directory; 8 Copy; 9 Find; N Name Search: 6
```

Figure 20-2. Macro files shown on the list screen

As you create macros, it can be useful to keep your own list of macro names, descriptions, and uses. That way, you can easily remember the use of each macro.

Executing a Macro

Once you have defined a macro, you can use it. This is called "executing" a macro. (Breathe easy. The work's in the defining, not the execution.)

It is a good practice to execute a new macro right after you've defined it. That way, you can test to see whether it works the way you intended. If it doesn't, you can define it again (select 1 Replace when that option arises) or edit the macro (described in a minute).

> ▶ **Hint:** It is a good habit to save your document *before*
> executing a macro. That way, if you have valuable
> text and macro that doesn't execute properly, you don't
> lose the text.

To execute the macro, place your cursor where you want
to insert the macro. Then press Alt-F10 Macro or select Macro,
then Execute from the Tools menu. This message appears:

```
Macro:
```

Type in the macro name and press Enter or press the
Alt-letter key combination. The macro replays. If there is existing text, text in the macro is inserted at the position of the
cursor.

Figure 20-3 shows a letter before our BRETADD.WPM
macro is executed, and Figure 20-4 shows the letter after the
macro is executed. Notice that the text is inserted in existing
text. No editing of the document had to be done in this example. Often, however, you may need to add extra lines or
spaces after executing a macro to create the proper appearance.

217

```
  File Edit Search Layout Mark Tools Font Graphics Help

  Mr. David Randolph
  Bennington Corporation
  45 Superstition Highway
  Phoenix, Arizona 85252

                          May 12, 1991


  Dear Mr. Randolph:

       As I discussed, I am very interested in
  pursuing a career with the Bennington
  Corporation.  I have attached:

       o    My resume with a chronological work
            history as requested
       o    Letters of recommendation
       o    Certificates of achievement

       Your friend, Jim Miller, recently ap-
  plauded my work on our exposition with these
  remarks at the dinner presentation:
  C:\WP51\DOC\BELET.WPP            Doc 1 Pg 1 Ln 1" Pos 2"
```

Figure 20-3. Letter before executing macro

```
File Edit Search Layout Mark Tools Font Graphics Help
━━━━━━━━━━━━━━━━━━━━━━━━━━━━━━━━━━━━━━━━━━━━━━━━━━━━━━━━━━━━
                     Barbara J. Wiley
                      3421 Pecos Way
                 San Diego, California 92123

Mr. David Randolph
Bennington Corporation
45 Superstition Highway
Phoenix, Arizona 85252

                            May 12, 1991


Dear Mr. Randolph:

     As I discussed, I am very interested in
pursuing a career with the Bennington
Corporation.  I have attached:

        o     My resume with a chronological work
              history as requested
        o     Letters of recommendation
        o     Certificates of achievement
C:\WP51\DOC\BELET.WPP                 Doc 1 Pg 1 Ln 1.5" Pos 2"
```

Figure 20-4. Letter after executing macro

Q Macro Execution

1. Position the cursor where the macro should execute and press Alt-F10 Macro, or select Macro, then Execute from the Tools menu.

   This messages appears:
   `Macro:`

2. Type in the macro name and press Enter or press the Alt-letter key combination.

   The macro keystrokes execute.

Editing a Macro

When you edit a macro, an editing screen like that shown in Figure 20-5 appears. In this screen, the name of the macro (the file), the macro description, and all the keystrokes appear. Each Word-Perfect command appears in braces ({}). For example, the Shift-F6

Center command appears as {Center} and a press of the Enter key appears as {Enter}. Text you have typed in appears as text and spaces are represented by dots or small, underlined circles. Notice in the figure that a typographical error was made and corrected when the macro was defined: "San Diego" was misspelled as "San Dieb," Backspace was pressed, and "go" was entered.

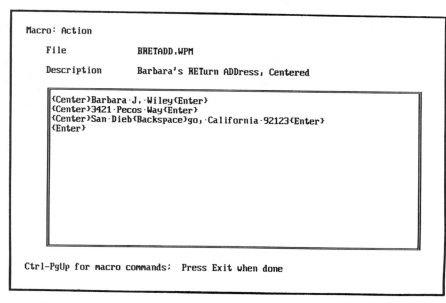

Figure 20-5. Macro editing screen

When you edit a macro, you can correct errors or add new text or keypresses. Just press Ctrl-F10 Macro Define or select Macro, then Define from the Tools menu. Enter the name of the existing macro you want to edit (press Enter, if necessary). A message like this is displayed:

BRETADD.WPM Already Exists: 1 Replace; 2 Edit; 3 Description:

To edit the description and the keystrokes, press *3* Description. Make any changes to the description, press Enter, and edit the keystrokes. To edit the keystrokes only, press *2* Edit.

When you edit keystrokes, you can use most WordPerfect editing commands. Just delete text you don't want and insert the text you want to add. To add a WordPerfect keypress, enter the appropriate WordPerfect keystrokes. In Figure 20-6, the "b" and {Backspace} have been deleted to correct the typographical error.

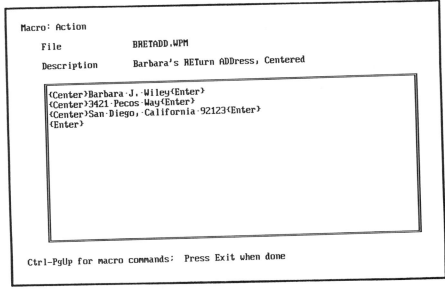

```
Macro: Action

    File                BRETADD.WPM

    Description         Barbara's RETurn ADDress, Centered

    {Center}Barbara·J.·Wiley{Enter}
    {Center}3421·Pecos·Way{Enter}
    {Center}San·Diego,·California·92123{Enter}
    {Enter}
```

Ctrl-PgUp for macro commands: Press Exit when done

Figure 20-6. Edited BRETADD.WPM macro

During editing, you can press F1 Cancel to leave the macro as it was and return to your document. This message appears for your response:

Cancel Changes? No (Yes)

Press *y* to cancel any edits and return to your document. Press *n* to go back to editing the macro.

Once your editing is complete, press F7 Exit to save the changes. You are returned to your document.

 Hint: After editing a macro, always test it to make sure it executes as you anticipated.

220

Q Editing a Macro

1. Press Ctrl-F10 Macro Define or select Macro, then Define from the Tools menu.

   This message appears:
   `Define Macro:`

2. Enter the name of the existing macro.

   These options appear:
   `1 Replace; 2 Edit;`
   `3 Description`

3. Press *2* Edit to edit the keystrokes only or *3* Description to edit the description and keystrokes.

   The appropriate macro information appears.

4. Edit the text. After editing, press F7 Exit.

   You are returned to your document.

□ **221**

For Your Information

This chapter has just scratched the surface of the potential of macros. In addition to entering keystrokes and WordPerfect operations, you could include a variety of special contents in your macros. These include macro programming commands, expressions, and message display commands. They are the means to add to your macro intelligence beyond typical WordPerfect capabilities.

For example, you could add the WordPerfect programming command {Bell} through the macro editing screen to sound a bell. You could add pauses to enter text from the keyboard, prompts to remind you of actions to take, or use If-Else statements to make choices.

These are only a few of the possibilities WordPerfect provides. First get some experience with the level of macro work described in this chapter. Then consult the WordPerfect manual or an advanced book on WordPerfect to learn about these more sophisticated macro functions.

Summary

In this chapter you've learned:

▶ Macros are used to automate repetitive tasks.

▶ To define a macro, press Ctrl-F10 Macro Define or select Macro and then Define from the Tools menu. Name the macro (eight or fewer letters or Alt with a letter). Enter a description and press Enter. Then enter the keystrokes. Press Ctrl-F10 Macro Define or select Macro, then Define from the Tools menu to complete the operation.

▶ To execute a macro, press Alt-F10 Macro or select Macro, then Execute from the Tools menu. Enter the name. The macro is played.

▶ To edit a macro, use the define-macro process and enter the name of the existing macro. Select 2 Edit (keystrokes only) or 3 Description (description and keystrokes) when prompted. Press F7 Exit when you are done editing the macro.

Chapter 21

Creating Tables of Contents, Indexes, and Outlines

In This Chapter

▶ *How to create a table of contents automatically*
▶ *How to generate an index*
▶ *How to develop an outline*

Benefits of "Automated" Tables of Contents and Indexes

The "old fashioned" way of creating a table of contents or an index is to identify the text manually in your document after all page numbers have been assigned and then type in each entry along with the page number. If the document is edited and the page numbers change, the table of contents and index have to be updated manually.

With WordPerfect, the process of creating tables of contents and indexes is greatly simplified. In the document, you mark the text that is to be included in the table of contents or index. Then generate the table of contents or index automatically. When the document is edited, generate the references again. There's no manual record-keeping of what's in the index and table of contents and no manual updating of the table of contents and index. And there is no chance of errors relative to page numbering.

Steps to Creating a Table of Contents or Index

To create a table of contents or index, follow these basic steps:

224

1. Mark the text you want to include in the table of contents or index: This identifies to WordPerfect the entries for the table of contents or index.
2. Define the characteristics of the table of contents or index: You can identify the location and appearance of a table of contents and the location for index words.
3. Generate the table of contents and/or index: WordPerfect finds each occurrence of the text marked for a table of contents and/or index and creates the references.

Marking and Defining a Table of Contents

You may create a table of contents with from one to five levels. Each additional level is a "sublevel." Figure 21-1 shows part of a table of contents for a document created by Barbara J. Wiley. It has only one level. Figure 21-2 shows a portion of Wiley's table of contents, this time with two levels. Each new sublevel in a table of contents is indented to the next tab stop.

To mark an entry for a table of contents, use Alt-F4 Block to block the text to be included. Once the entry is blocked, press

```
                   Developing a Computer System
                By Barbara J. Wiley and Paul G. Otto

     Table of Contents

     Major Tasks. . . . . . . . . . . . . . . . . . . . . . 1
     Specification. . . . . . . . . . . . . . . . . . . . . 7
     Design . . . . . . . . . . . . . . . . . . . . . . . 13
     Coding . . . . . . . . . . . . . . . . . . . . . . . 19
     Implementation . . . . . . . . . . . . . . . . . . . 26
     Post Implementation. . . . . . . . . . . . . . . . . 34
```

225

Figure 21-1. Table of contents with one level

```
                   Developing a Computer System
                By Barbara J. Wiley and Paul G. Otto

     Table of Contents

     Major Tasks. . . . . . . . . . . . . . . . . . . . . . 1
          Specification . . . . . . . . . . . . . . . . . . 2
          Design. . . . . . . . . . . . . . . . . . . . . . 3
          Coding. . . . . . . . . . . . . . . . . . . . . . 3
          Implementation. . . . . . . . . . . . . . . . . . 5
          Post Implementation . . . . . . . . . . . . . . . 6
     Specification. . . . . . . . . . . . . . . . . . . . . 7
          The Goal. . . . . . . . . . . . . . . . . . . . . 8
          User Requirements . . . . . . . . . . . . . . . . 8
          The Role of MIS . . . . . . . . . . . . . . . . 10
     Design . . . . . . . . . . . . . . . . . . . . . . . 13
          The Goal. . . . . . . . . . . . . . . . . . . . 13
          The Team. . . . . . . . . . . . . . . . . . . . 15
          The Detail System Design Document . . . . . . . 18
```

Figure 21-2. Table of contents with two levels

Alt-F5 Mark Text and press *1* ToC (Table of Contents). Or select Table of Contents from the Mark menu. Type in the number of levels (1 through 5). Codes like these surround the text:

```
[Mark:ToC,1]Major Tasks[End Mark:ToC,1]
```

The type of mark is shown (ToC for Table of Contents), along with the number of levels (in this case, 1). Continue the process of marking table of contents entries until all entries are marked.

Q Mark Table of Contents Entry

1.	Block the entry with Alt-F4 Block.	The entry for the table of contents is identified.
2.	Press Alt-F5 Mark Text and *1* ToC, or select Table of Contents from the Mark menu.	The level option is available.
3.	Enter the level (1, 2, 3, 4, or 5).	Codes are placed around the text.

Once all table of contents entries are marked, you must define the table of contents. Place your cursor where you want the table of contents to appear. Typically, you will want it at the beginning of the document on its own page. (To create a page, enter a hard page break with Ctrl-Enter.) You may also enter a heading, such as a simple "Contents."

To define the table of contents, press Alt-F5 Mark Text, *5* Define, then *1* Table of Contents. Or select Define, then Table of Contents from the Mark menu. The Table of Contents Definition screen (see Figure 21-3) appears.

Identify the number of levels by pressing *1* Number of Levels and typing in the number. Leave option 2 Display Last Level in Wrapped Format at No. (Otherwise the levels wrap around as if they are part of one paragraph.) Select *3* Page Numbering to choose how page numbers are to be displayed:

1 None (no page numbers). For example:
   Major Tasks
2 Page number follows text:
   Major Tasks 1

```
┌──────────────────────────────────────────────────────────────┐
│                                                                │
│    Table of Contents Definition                               │
│                                                                │
│        1 - Number of Levels          1                        │
│                                                                │
│        2 - Display Last Level in      No                      │
│              Wrapped Format                                    │
│                                                                │
│        3 - Page Numbering - Level 1  Flush right with leader  │
│                            Level 2                             │
│                            Level 3                             │
│                            Level 4                             │
│                            Level 5                             │
│                                                                │
│                                                                │
│                                                                │
│                                                                │
│                                                                │
│                                                                │
│    Selection: 0                                               │
│                                                                │
└──────────────────────────────────────────────────────────────┘
```

227

Figure 21-3. Table of Contents Definition screen

3 Page number in parentheses follows text:
   Major Tasks (1)
4 Page number flush right:
   Major Tasks   1
5 Page number flush right with dot leaders:
   Major Tasks 1

Press F7 Exit when you are done. A code like this appears in your document:

```
[Def Mark:ToC,3:5,5,5]
```

Translation: Definition mark for table of contents. There are three levels and the page numbering on each level is set to choice 5 (flush right with dot leaders).

    Once you have marked the table of contents entries and defined the table of contents, you can generate it, which is discussed in "Generating the Table of Contents and/or Index" later in this chapter. Because you generate both the table of contents and index at the same time, you may want to mark and define an index first.

Marking and Defining an Index

When you create an index, you can use headings and subheadings. Figure 21-4 shows a portion of an index with headings and subheadings. Notice that the subheadings are indented under the associated heading. The tab stops are used for indentation.

228

```
Index

ABC Approach . . . . . . . . . . . . . . . . . . . . . . . .  2
Benefits to Users. . . . . . . . . . . . . . . . . . . . . .  1
BITTLE Company Experience. . . . . . . . . . . . . . . . . . 54
Coding . . . . . . . . . . . . . . . . . . . . . . . . . . . 19
       Common Problems and Solutions . . . . . . . . . . . . 24
       Handling DSD Changes. . . . . . . . . . . . . . . . . 21
       Managing the Coding Activity. . . . . . . . . . . . . 25
       Methods to Code . . . . . . . . . . . . . . . . . . . 22
Cutting Costs. . . . . . . . . . . . . . . . . . . . . . . . 42
```

Figure 21-4. Index with headings and subheadings

To mark a single word as an index entry, place your cursor on that word. To mark several words making up one entry, block (Alt-F4 Block) the words. Positioning the cursor marks the text to use to identify the page number. As you will see, you can change the actual wording of the index entry, if desired.

Press Alt-F5 Mark Text and type *3* Index, or select Index from the Mark menu. This prompt appears:

`Index heading:`

The word(s) you've identified appear after the prompt. Press Enter to use the text as marked or type in your own index entry. (For instance, you may want different capitalization, a different tense, or entirely different text.) Press Enter. This prompt appears:

`Subheading:`

Press F1 Cancel if you don't want a subheading. If you want one, either type in a subheading and press Enter or just accept the one shown by pressing Enter. Codes are placed in your document around the marked word(s). Here is an example:

`[Index:Coding;Common Problems and Solutions]`

In this example, the heading is "Coding" and the subheading is "Common Problems and Solutions."

229

Q Mark an Index Entry

1. Place your cursor on the word or block the words for the entry using Alt-F4 Block.

   The page number for the index entry is identified.

2. Press Alt-F5 Mark Text, then *3* Index, or select Index from the Mark menu.

   This prompt appears:
   `Index heading:`

3. Accept the heading or enter a new one. Press Enter.

   This prompt appears:
   `Subheading:`

4. Accept the subheading or enter a new one. Press Enter. Or press F1 Cancel to skip the subheading.

   Codes appear in your document.

There is one other method to use in identifying words for an index. You can create a *concordance file*, which is a list of words you want in the index. WordPerfect looks for and marks these words in your document. You can check each mark, adding and deleting marks as desired. For more information on using a concordance file, see your WordPerfect manual.

Once all index entries are marked, define the index. To do so, place your cursor where you want the index to appear in your document. Press Alt-F5 Mark Text, *5* Define, and *3* Define Index, or select Define then Index from the Mark menu. This prompt appears:

Concordance Filename (Enter=none):

Press Enter (this assumes you are not using a concordance file) and the Index Definition screen (see Figure 21-5) appears.

230

```
Index Definition

     1 - No Page Numbers

     2 - Page Numbers Follow Entries

     3 - (Page Numbers) Follow Entries

     4 - Flush Right Page Numbers

     5 - Flush Right Page Numbers with Leaders








Selection: 0
```

Figure 21-5. Index Definition screen

These are the options:

1 No page numbers. For example:
    Coding
2 Page numbers follow entries:
    Coding 19

3 Page numbers in parentheses follow entries:
Coding (19)
4 Page numbers flush right on the page:
Coding   19
5 Page numbers flush right on the page with dot leaders:
Coding 19

Once you've selected how the page numbers will appear, a code like this is placed in your document:

[Def Mark:Index,5]

This identifies where the index will be placed and the type of page numbering. (In this example, option 5 was selected: flush right with dot leaders.)

Generating the Table of Contents and/or Index

231

To generate the table of contents and/or index, press Alt-F5 Mark Text and *6* Generate. Or select Generate from the Mark menu. The Mark: Generate screen appears. Select *5* Generate Tables, Indexes, Cross-References, etc. This prompt appears:

Existing tables, lists, and indexes will be replaced. Continue? Yes (No)

To continue, press *y* for Yes. A prompt like this identifies that the work is being done:

Generation in progress. Pass: 1, Page: 9

When the prompt goes away, the table of contents and index have been generated. The table of contents or index appears after the appropriate [Def Mark: . . .]. Following the table of contents or index, this code appears:

[End Def]

⊘ **Caution:** Never delete the [Def Mark: . . .] or [End Def] codes. If you do, WordPerfect will not know where to put the table of contents or index if you generate it again. Only delete these codes if you are deleting the entire table of contents or index.

Once the table of contents or index has been generated, you can edit it like any document text. For example, you may add your own headings, blank lines, or change tab stops to alter the indentation.

▶ **Hint:** You will usually want to generate your table of contents and index after spell checking but before printing your document. This way, all editing will be complete and the page numbers will be stable. Sometimes, however, it is useful to generate the table of contents and/or index as you work. Doing so provides a reference to see the structure of the document and the location of particular material. You can generate a table of contents and index again and again.

For Your Information

As you strolled through the prompts and menus for creating a table of contents and index, your curiosity may have been raised about several other WordPerfect features.

You can use WordPerfect to create *cross references*. Cross references refer the reader to another page in the document. For example, you can say:

See the chart on page 27 for an overview.

Or...

Page 34 describes the steps in detail.

The text you use in the cross reference is up to you. What WordPerfect offers is automatic updating of the page number every time it changes as a result of editing the document.

Another feature is the ability to develop *tables of authorities*. These are used in legal documents to cite statutes, cases, and legal references.

You can also use WordPerfect to create a *master document* in one WordPerfect document file (with or without text). This master document "calls" other documents. The master document can be expanded to include all subdocuments or condensed to include only itself. The benefit of this feature is that you may create small, workable document files and then expand them to one large document file for final editing.

Finally, you may have noticed the references to redline and strikeout. These features, described in Chapter 14, are useful for editing documents when more than one person is involved in the editing process.

233

Creating Outlines

Outlining is another useful organizing technique WordPerfect makes easy. You can go into outline mode and the text you type in will be automatically numbered and indented; you don't have to remember what number or letter comes next or how far to indent. Also, numbers and letters are automatically updated when you edit the outline. Figure 21-6 illustrates part of an outline created using WordPerfect.

To develop an outline, put the cursor where the outline will start. Press Shift-F5 Date/Outline and press *4* Outline, or select Outline from the Tools menu. Choose On to turn on Outline. This code appears in your document:

```
[Outline On]
```

"Outline" appears in the lower left corner of your screen to remind you that you are in Outline mode. From here until you turn Outline Off, text you enter will be in outline form. As you will see, while in Outline mode, certain keypresses give different results in Outline mode than when you are in regular editing mode.

```
Talk for Data Processing Professional Group
By Barbara J. Wiley

I.   Background of presenters
II.  Why computer systems haven't met needs
III. Benefits of a better approach
IV.  Major tasks
     A.   Specification
          1.   The stated and hidden goals
          2.   Getting user requirements
          3.   Story of BITTLE
          4.   MIS role (new and old)
     B.   Design
```

Figure 21-6. An outline created with WordPerfect

234

Press Enter to have the first-level number inserted. Type in text or, to go to the next level, press Tab. To go back a level, use Shift-Tab Margin Release. Continue using these keys while you create your outline. Here is a summary of the keys to press and the results:

Key to press	Result
Enter	To create a new line at the same level
Tab	To go "in" (right) one level
Shift-Tab Margin Release	To go "out" (left) one level

When you insert a level number, a code for paragraph numbering appears in the text:

[Para Num: Auto]

For example, in Figure 21-6, Outlining was turned on after the outline title and Barbara J. Wiley's by-line. The first line was automatically numbered I. The text was typed in. After pressing Enter at the end of the line, II appears. That line was typed in. The same approach was used for lines III and IV. After pressing Enter at the end of line IV, V appeared. To go to a new level, Tab was pressed. The V disappeared and A appeared. "Specification" was typed in. Then, Enter, followed by Tab, was pressed to go to a new level, level 1. From the line marked 1 through the line marked 4, Enter was pressed at the end of the line because each line is at the same level. After line 4, 5 appeared. Shift-Tab was pressed to move left one tab stop. The 5 was replaced by B.

> ▶ **Hint:** Outlining can feel a little cumbersome at first. Most people new to creating outlines take a few minutes to experiment with the keypresses to get the hang of the actions. Once you become familiar with the results, you'll pick up speed.

When you are done creating the outline, press Shift-F5 Date/Outline, then press *4* Outline. Or select Outline from the Tools menu. Choose Off to turn Outline off and return to regular editing mode. "Outline" disappears from the screen and a code [Outline Off] appears in the document.

Q Creating an Outline

1. Place your cursor where you want the outline to begin. Press Shift-F5 Date/Outline, *4* Outline, and *1* On, or select Outline, then On from the Tools menu.

   A code is placed in the document and Outline appears on the screen.

2. Type in the outline. Press Enter to keep the same level, Tab to go right a level, or Shift-Tab to go left a level.

   The outline is created.

3. Press Shift-F5 Date/Outline, *4* Outline, and *2* Off, or select Outline, then Off from the Tools menu.

   A code is inserted. You are returned to regular document-editing mode.

This description of outlining will get you started. Consult your WordPerfect manual if you use outlining often and want to learn a few tricks. For example, there are keypresses that move you more than one level at a time and to the most recent occurrence of the same level. Also, you may use the Move/Copy/Delete options to control a level of the outline and all subordinate levels. In addition, you can use the Outline, Define function to change the style of outline numbers, to begin outlining with any number, and to alter the use of the Enter key.

For Your Information

During your exploration of the outlining function, you ran into some other WordPerfect options. This is a brief explanation of those options. See your WordPerfect manual for a complete description of them if you believe they will be useful in your work.

WordPerfect allows you to number paragraphs. The numbering scheme is similar to what you have seen with outlining.

Another interesting feature is that WordPerfect will automatically enter the date (actually, the system date entered in your computer). You can use Shift-F5 Date/Outline and then one of these options (or select one from the Tools menu):

1 Date Text: To enter the date in letters and numbers
2 Date Code: To place a code that will add the current date every time you enter or print the document
3 Date Format: To change the appearance of the date, add the day, or add the time (for example, November 26, 1989 to Sun Nov 26, 1989)

Summary

In this chapter you've learned:

▶ To create a table of contents and/or index, mark each entry, define it, then generate it.

▶ To mark either a table of contents or index entry, identify the entry. Press Alt-F5 Mark Text or select the Mark menu. Continue according to the type of entry you are marking.

▶ To define a table of contents or index, place your cursor in the reference location. Press Alt-F5 Mark Text, then 5 Define, or select Define from the Tools menu.

▶ To generate the table of contents or index, press Alt-F5 Mark Text and 6 Generate, or select Generate from the Mark menu. Select 5 Generate Tables, Indexes.

▶ To create an outline, use Shift-F5 Date/Outline or select Outline from the Tools menu. Turn the Outline feature On; use Enter, Tab, and Shift-Tab to control the outline entry; then turn Outline Off.

237

Merging Documents and Data

In this Chapter

▶ *Why merge documents and data?*
▶ *How to merge documents and data*

Why Merge Documents and Data?

WordPerfect allows you to merge the contents of one document with a list of data in another document. The data may comprise any small bits of information, such as names, addresses, telephone numbers, product numbers, sales regions, contributions, booth assignments, office numbers, birth dates . . . well, you get the idea.

What use is this feature to you? If you ever need to send out form letters or use the same data in multiple documents, the Merge feature will save you a great deal of time and enable you to produce more personalized letters and documents.

For example, you may merge a list of names, addresses, and phone numbers of members of a professional group, a work team, or a scout troop. Then you merge that data with a notice today, a letter tomorrow, or to make a list next week. Or you could create a document containing raw product data and then pull out the data you need according to the requirements of the immediate document. Virtually any time you have a body of data that you will be using repeatedly, Merge is the way to go.

Elements of a Merge

Each piece of data in a merge is referred to as a *field*. A field may be a first name, last name, phone number, zip code—any single bit of information. All the related fields are organized into a *record*. For example, all the fields for one person (first name, last name, address, phone number) are organized into a record for that individual.

240

Three documents are involved in a merge:

1. The *primary document*: This is the "boilerplate" text that will be used in the merged document. Type it in as regular WordPerfect text. In this document, you also identify what data you want "plugged in." By entering codes for the fields, you tell WordPerfect what to put where.

2. The *secondary document*: This document contains the data, organized in a way that WordPerfect can identify what's what. For example, the fields in each record are listed in the same order and the records are clearly separated. This way, WordPerfect knows what type of field comes first, second, third, and so on. And, WordPerfect knows where one record ends and another begins.

3. The *merged document*: This is the result of merging the primary document and secondary document. The data from the secondary document is entered at the appropriate spots according to the instructions in the primary document.

Let's take a look at an example of each type of document. We'll use Barbara Wiley's notice to the members of her professional group as the example. Figure 22-1 shows the primary document. Notice that each field to be substituted for during the merge is numbered and appears with a notation on the regular editing screen:

{FIELD}1~

On the Reveal Codes screen, you see:

[Mrg:FIELD]1~

which reminds you that the field is to be merged.

```
 File Edit Search Layout Mark Tools Font Graphics Help
 {FIELD}1~ {FIELD}2~
 {FIELD}3?~
 {FIELD}4~
 {FIELD}5~
 {FIELD}6~, TX {FIELD}7~

 Dear {FIELD}1~:

     Our annual conference is scheduled for May 23-25.  {FIELD}1~, are you
 C:\WP51\DOC\MAYPRIM.WPP                          Doc 1 Pg 1 Ln 2" Pos 1.8"
 [    ▲    ▲    ▲    ▲    ▲    ▲    ▲    ▲    ▲    ▲    ▲    }    ▲    ▲
 [Mrg:FIELD]5~[HRt]
 [Mrg:FIELD]6~, TX [Mrg:FIELD]7~[HRt]
 [HRt]
 Dear [Mrg:FIELD]1~:[HRt]
 [HRt]
 [Tab]Our annual conference is scheduled for May 23[-]25.  [Mrg:FIELD]1~, are you
 [SRt]
 interested in presenting a seminar?  Many successful seminars are[SRt]
 based on "real world" experiences.  How about your experience at[SRt]
 [Mrg:FIELD]4~?  If you can present a seminar, call me at 253[-]9900 extension[SR

 Press Reveal Codes to restore screen
```

Figure 22-1. Primary document

The full-screen display of our primary document, shown in Figure 22-2, illustrates that the order of the fields is not important. The numbers of the fields simply let WordPerfect match up with the proper data in the secondary document. Also, fields do not need to be represented an equal number of times in the primary document: Field 1 is used three times and field 4 is used twice.

Also notice that field 3 has a question mark after the number and before the tilde (~). This tells WordPerfect that not every record in the secondary document will have data for

```
File Edit Search Layout Mark Tools Font Graphics Help
{FIELD}1~ {FIELD}2~
{FIELD}3?~
{FIELD}4~
{FIELD}5~
{FIELD}6~, TX {FIELD}7~

Dear {FIELD}1~:

     Our annual conference is scheduled for May 23-25.  {FIELD}1~, are you
interested in presenting a seminar?  Many successful seminars are
based on "real world" experiences.  How about your experience at
{FIELD}4~?  If you can present a seminar, call me at 253-9900 extension
3050 (day) or 432-9822 (evening).  Thank you.

Sincerely,


Barbara J. Wiley




C:\WP51\DOC\MAYPRIM.WPP          Doc 1 Pg 1 Ln 3.83" Pos 2.6"
```

Figure 22-2. Full-screen display of primary document

field 3. If a record doesn't, field 3 will be skipped and no blank line will be left.

Now let's take a look at the secondary document. Figure 22-3 shows the full-screen display of several records. Notice that each field (such as first name) is entered on its own line and ends with:

{END FIELD}

The figure also shows that Jennifer Jackson's title is not available. A line is left as a placeholder to alert WordPerfect, but the {END FIELD} code is entered anyway. You can also see that there are more fields in the secondary document than are called for in the primary. The phone numbers, for example, appear in the secondary document but are not used in the primary document. This illustrates that you can use as much or as little data as you wish.

Take a look at the end of the record for Jennifer Jackson. The notation

{END RECORD}

signifies to WordPerfect that this record ends and the next

```
 File Edit Search Layout Mark Tools Font Graphics Help
 Jennifer<END FIELD>
 Jackson<END FIELD>
 <END FIELD>
 Williams Manufacturing<END FIELD>
 2344 W. Highway 1<END FIELD>
 San Diego<END FIELD>
 92123<END FIELD>
 342-8966<END FIELD>
 450-9000<END FIELD>
 <END RECORD>
=================================================================
 Preston<END FIELD>
 Lindermann<END FIELD>
 Analyst<END FIELD>
 Bottcher Ltd.<END FIELD>
 3422 45th Street<END FIELD>
 San Diego<END FIELD>
 92125<END FIELD>
 342-9877<END FIELD>
 234-2030<END FIELD>
 <END RECORD>
=================================================================
 Field: 1                              Doc 1 Pg 1 Ln 1" Pos 1"
```

243

Figure 22-3. Full-screen display of several records in a secondary document

record begins. WordPerfect automatically enters a hard page break for you.

Look at the order of the data in each record: the first name is always field 1, the last name is field 2, the title (or placeholder, if not present) is field 3, the company is field 4, and so on. The order in which your fields present data does not matter (for example, the last names could make up the first field). However, all records must have the fields in the same order by type and the same number of field lines. When this merge code is in the primary document

{FIELD}1~

the field 1 data is merged (in our example, the first name).

Figure 22-4 illustrates the codes as shown on the Reveal Codes screen. This code

[Mrg:END FIELD]

marks the end of each field. This code

[Mgr:END RECORD]

```
File Edit Search Layout Mark Tools Font Graphics Help
───────────────────────────────────────────────────────────
Jackson{END FIELD}
{END FIELD}
Williams Manufacturing{END FIELD}
2344 W. Highway 1{END FIELD}
San Diego{END FIELD}
92123{END FIELD}
342-8966{END FIELD}
450-9000{END FIELD}
{END RECORD}
Field: 4                              Doc 1 Pg 1 Ln 1.5" Pos 1"
[  ▲   ▲   ▲   ▲  [  ▲    ▲   ▲   ▲   ▲   ▲   ▲   }  ▲   ▲
Jennifer[Mrg:END FIELD][HRt]
Jackson[Mrg:END FIELD][HRt]
[Mrg:END FIELD][HRt]
Williams Manufacturing[Mrg:END FIELD][HRt]
2344 W. Highway 1[Mrg:END FIELD][HRt]
San Diego[Mrg:END FIELD][HRt]
92123[Mrg:END FIELD][HRt]
342[-]8966[Mrg:END FIELD][HRt]
450[-]9000[Mrg:END FIELD][HRt]
[Mrg:END RECORD][HPg]

Press Reveal Codes to restore screen
```

Figure 22-4. Secondary document Reveal Codes screen

marks the end of each record. Notice that a hard return ([HRt]) is also entered after the end of a record.

Figure 22-5 shows the first document (for Jennifer Jackson) fully merged, and it shows the beginning of the merging of the second document (for Preston Lindermann). The result of the merge, then, is one or more documents with the applicable fields from each record in the secondary merged into the primary document. You can edit or print the merged document.

Creating a Secondary Document

It's usually a good idea to create the secondary document (the one that lists the data) first. That way, when you create the primary document, you have established the field references in your organization of the secondary document.

Start with a blank WordPerfect screen. Type in the first data field (such as a name). When the field is entered, press F9 Merge R. {END FIELD} appears in your document screen and [Mrg:END FIELD] appears in the Reveal Codes screen. Press

```
 File Edit Search Layout Mark Tools Font Graphics Help

 Jennifer Jackson
 Williams Manufacturing
 2344 W. Highway 1
 San Diego, TX 92123

 Dear Jennifer:

     Our annual conference is scheduled for May 23-25. Jennifer,
 are you interested in presenting a seminar? Many successful
 seminars are based on "real world" experiences. How about your
 experience at Williams Manufacturing? If you can present a
 seminar, call me at 253-9900 extension 3050 (day) or 432-9822
 (evening). Thank you.

 Sincerely,


 Barbara J. Wiley
 ==============================================================================
 Preston Lindermann
 Analyst
 Bottcher Ltd.
 C:\WP51\DOC\MAYMERGE.WPP                       Doc 1 Pg 1 Ln 1" Pos 1"
```

Figure 22-5. Merged document

Enter to start a new line. Type in that second field, then press F9 Merge R. Remember, if you don't have data for a certain field in a record, press F9 Merge R to keep the line as a space holder.

As you work, notice that a prompt like this appears at the bottom of your screen:

Field: 1

This identifies the number assigned to the field on which your cursor rests. This is the number to use in the primary document to refer to the field.

When you have entered all the fields for one record, press Shift-F9 Merge Codes and *2* End Record. Or select Merge Codes, then End Record from the Tools menu. {END RECORD} appears on the document screen followed by a page break. [Mrg:END RECORD] appears in the Reveal Codes screen along with a [HRt] code for the hard return page break. Your cursor is placed past the page break and this prompt appears, instructing you to enter Field 1:

Field: 1

Continue entering fields and records in this manner until all are entered. Make sure to end the last record with {END RECORD}. Then save the document as you would any Word-Perfect document.

Q Create a Secondary Document

1. Enter the first field data and press F9 Merge R and then Enter.

   {END FIELD} appears and you are on a new line to enter another field. The number for the new field appears in the lower left of the screen.

2. Enter all the fields for a record following the process in step 1. On the line after the last field for the record, press Shift-F9 Merge Codes and *2* End Record, or select Merge Codes and End Record from the Tools menu.

   {END RECORD} and a hard page break are entered.

3. Enter the field for the next record. Or, if you are done entering records, save the document like any WordPerfect document.

   After saving the secondary document, you may use it in a merge.

246

Before leaving the secondary document for good, check the field entries and the end of each record carefully. Answer these questions: Does each record have the same number of fields? Are the types of fields in the same order in each record? Is there an {END FIELD} mark at the end of each field? Is there an {END RECORD} mark at the end of each record (including the last record)? Are there unnecessary blank lines or text that should be deleted?

> **⊘ Caution:** When entering the end field and end record codes, don't type in {END FIELD} or {END RECORD}. You *must* use the appropriate WordPerfect keypresses or menu selections.

Creating a Primary Document

To create a primary document, type in the boilerplate text. When you want to reference a field, press Shift-F9 Merge Codes and *1* Field, or select Merge Codes and then Field from the Tools menu. This prompt appears:

Enter Field:

Type in the number assigned to the field (in the secondary document) and press Enter. The entry looks like this:

{FIELD}1~

Again, don't type in {FIELD}1~ from your keyboard. If you do, that text will print, and you will not be calling data from the secondary document. You *must* use the WordPerfect keypresses or menu selections.

Continue to type in the boilerplate text and enter fields as desired. As mentioned earlier, fields need not be entered in order, and you can use all of the fields in the secondary document or only a few. When you are done creating the primary document, save it like any other WordPerfect document.

247

Q Create a Primary Document

1. Type in the boilerplate text. When you want to insert a field from the secondary document, press Shift-F9 Merge Codes and select *1* Field, or select Merge Codes and Field from the Tools menu. Type in the number of the field and press Enter.

   A code like this appears in your text: {FIELD}1~

2. When all text and fields are entered, save the document.

   The document is saved.

   ☐

Be sure to check your document before saving: Have you entered each field with the correct number? Is the punctuation placed appropriately around the field data that will be inserted?

Merging

Once you have completed the primary and secondary documents, you can merge them. Start with a blank WordPerfect screen. Press Ctrl-F9 Merge/Sort then *1* Merge, or select Merge from the Tools menu. This prompt appears:

Primary file:

248   Type in the name of the primary file (include the drive and path, if necessary) and press Enter. This prompt appears:

Secondary file:

Type in, as needed, the drive, path, and name of the secondary document. Press Enter and the merge begins. This prompt tells you that WordPerfect is merging the two documents:

* Merging *

The documents are merged and appear on your screen. Check to make sure the result is as you expected. Save the document. You may edit it and print it as you would any WordPerfect document.

▶ **Hint:** When you begin using merge, your first results may not come out as you wanted. This is pretty normal. Call up the secondary document and check each record and field carefully. Then look at your primary document and check each field carefully. Pay special attention to the fields and records where the data did not print appropriately. After making corrections, try again.

For Your Information

We've just touched on the basics of the power of WordPerfect's merge capabilities. Master these first, and then consult a more advanced book on WordPerfect to learn how to perform other activities, including:

▶ Assign field names in place of numbers to make your primary documents more descriptive

▶ Pause the merge in order to enter data from the keyboard for one-time data needs

▶ Insert the current date

▶ Start a macro from the end of a merge to perform another activity

▶ Print all the records from a secondary document on one page (to create lists of members, for example)

▶ Display a message as you merge

▶ Insert a document file instead of identifying a primary file

▶ Stop the merge at a certain point (for example, to merge only part of the data in a secondary document)

249

Summary

In this chapter you've learned:

▶ Fields for records are entered in a secondary document. To end a field, press F9 Merge R. To end a record, press Shift-F9 Merge Codes and 2 End Record, or select Merge Codes then End Record from the Tools menu.

▶ Boilerplate text and field codes are entered in the primary document. To identify a field to merge, press Shift-F9 Merge Codes and 1 Field, or select Merge Codes and Field from the Tools menu. Type in the correct number for the field you want and press Enter.

▶ To merge the primary and secondary documents, either press Ctrl-F9 Merge/Sort and 1 Merge or select Merge from the Tools menu. Enter the name of the primary and secondary documents and watch the merge take place.

250

Math and Tables

In This Chapter

▶ *How to perform math*
▶ *How to use tables*

Math

WordPerfect allows you to perform simple math functions automatically. If you are placing a few numbers in a document and want to use WordPerfect instead of a calculator, you can use the Math function. If you'll be needing a more advanced math capability (for instance, working with many numbers in rows and columns), use WordPerfect's Tables function (described later in this chapter).

When you use Math, you'll enter values at the tab stops and calculate down for subtotals, totals, and grand totals. As an example, we'll see how Barbara's document (see Figure 23-1) handles math. It calculates the staff hours required for different project phases, producing subtotals and a total of all subtotals and integrating the math with the document text.

```
File Edit Search Layout Mark Tools Font Graphics Help
                      Programmer      Analyst         Manager
                      Hours           Hours           Hours
Specification          34.00          101.50          100.00
Design                 68.50          203.00           88.50
Coding                290.00           30.00           20.50
   Subtotal           392.50+         334.50+         201.00+

Implementation        190.50           20.00           40.50
Post Implementation    56.00           10.00           70.00
   Subtotal           246.50+          30.00+         110.50+

   Total of Subtotals 639.00=         364.50=         311.50=

The calculations shown here identify the spread of hours from three
classifications of staff: Programmer, Analyst, and Manager.  Hours
spent by Users were not maintained but are estimated in the
discussion that follows.




Math                                      Doc 1 Pg 1 Ln 1.5" Pos 1"
```

Figure 23-1. Completed math calculation

Using Math

To use Math, place the cursor in the desired document location. When you use WordPerfect to perform math, the tab stops are automatically used as decimal tabs. Set tab stops now as desired.

Turn on math by pressing Alt-F7 Columns/Tables and *3* Math and then *1* On. Or select Math and then On from the Layout menu. This code is placed in your document:

[Math On]

Also, <<Math>> appears in the bottom left of the screen when your cursor is right of the [Math On] code.

Enter the numbers under any tab stop. Press Tab to move between tab stops and Enter to complete a line. To identify the math to be performed, enter the appropriate operator, from among those shown in Table 23-1, on a line in the column.

Table 23-1. Math operators

Symbol to enter	Code in document	Purpose
+	[+]	Subtotals the numbers above the + sign
=	[=]	Totals all the subtotals above the = sign
*	[*]	Gives a grand total of the totals above the sign

Figure 23-2 shows the placement of Barbara's figures before calculation. Notice the placement of the symbols: Symbols for subtotals and totals of subtotals are placed at tab stops under the number column.

```
File Edit Search Layout Mark Tools Font Graphics Help

                    Programmer      Analyst       Manager
                    Hours           Hours         Hours

Specification       34.00           101.50        100.00
Design              68.50           203.00        80.50
Coding              290.00          30.00         20.50
   Subtotal         +               +             +

Implementation      190.50          20.00         40.50
Post Implementation 56.00           10.00         70.00
   Subtotal         +               +             +

   Total of Subtotals  =               =             =

The calculations shown here identify the spread of hours from three
classifications of staff: Programmer, Analyst, and Manager.  Hours
spent by Users were not maintained but are estimated in the
discussion that follows.




C:\WP51\DOC\23-2                        Doc 1 Pg 1 Ln 1" Pos 1"
```

Figure 23-2. Setup prior to calculation

Once all the entries are made, to perform the calculation, press Alt-F7 Columns/Tables, *3* Math, and *4* Calculate. Or select Math and then Calculate from the Layout menu. The calculations are displayed.

When you are done with the math, turn it off. Press Alt-F7 Columns/Tables, *3* Math, and *2* Off. Or select Math and Off from the Layout menu. This code is placed in your document:

[Math Off]

The <<Math>> prompt disappears from your screen and you are in regular document-editing mode.

Q Using Math

1. Press Alt-F7 Columns/ Tables, *3* Math, and *1* On, or select Math and On from the Layout menu.

The [Math On] code is placed in your document.

2. Type in numbers under tab stops. Enter + for subtotals, = for totals of subtotals, and * for grand totals of totals.

The numbers and symbols are laid out.

3. Press Alt-F7 Columns/ Tables, *3* Math, and *4* Calculate, or select Math and Calculate from the Layout menu.

The calculation is performed.

4. Press Alt-F7 Columns/ Tables, *3* Math, and *2* Off, or select Math and Off from the Format menu.

Math is turned off.

For more sophisticated math requirements, you could use the Math Define function, which is accessed either through Alt-F7 Columns/Tables, 3 Math, and 3 Define or Math and then Define on the Layout menu. This feature allows you to calculate across instead of down, enter text in columns, control the number of digits to the right of the decimal, and enter formulas. However, my advice is to put your time to better use learning to use WordPerfect's tables function. It allows you to do all that and more.

Tables

Using WordPerfect's Tables function allows you to set up rows and columns and perform math calculations much as you can with a spreadsheet (such as the popular Lotus 1-2-3). Figure 23-3 shows tables from Barbara's work. The *columns* are the horizontal boxes. Think of them as being assigned letters, starting with A at the far left, then B, and so on. The *rows* are vertical boxes. Think of them as being assigned numbers, with the first row 1, the second row 2, and so on. Each box is referred to as a *cell*. This way, you can refer to a particular cell by letter and then number. For example, in the figure, the cell with the number 45,650.00 is cell B2. When the cursor is in the cell, as in the figure, the cell reference appears in the status line at the bottom right of the screen.

```
File Edit Search Layout Mark Tools Font Graphics Help
```

	Quarter One	Quarter Two	Total	% Saved
Salaries	45,650.00	35,899.00	81,549.00	21.36
Office	3,400.00	3,400.00	6,800.00	0.00
Telephone	1,987.45	1,798.08	3,785.53	9.53
Travel	1,098.42	235.90	1,334.32	78.52
Supplies	2,436.90	1,700.93	4,137.83	30.20
Temporary	9,943.88	19,934.09	29,877.97	-100.47
Equipment	19,048.98	12,978.92	32,027.90	31.87
Total	83,565.63	75,946.92	159,512.55	9.12

```
=B10-C10/B10*100                    Cell E10 Doc 1 Pg 1 Ln 3.83" Pos 6.98"
```

Figure 23-3. Math performed with the Tables feature

Creating a Table

To begin creating a table, position your cursor at the left margin. Choose the position that will be the top left of the table. Press Alt-F7 Columns/Tables, *2* Tables, and *1* Create, or select Tables and then Create from the Layout menu. This prompt appears:

Number of columns:

Type in the number of columns and press Enter. This prompt appears:

Number of rows:

Type in the number of rows and press Enter. WordPerfect makes a row the width of one line and calculates even column widths based on the space available between the margins you have set. A grid like that shown in Figure 23-4 appears. Features for editing the size and appearance of the table and to perform math appear at the bottom of the screen. For now, let's go on and develop the table.

256

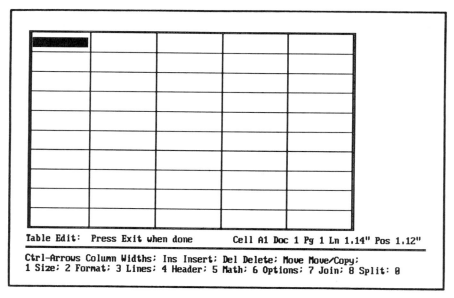

```
Table Edit:   Press Exit when done        Cell A1 Doc 1 Pg 1 Ln 1.14" Pos 1.12"

Ctrl-Arrows Column Widths; Ins Insert; Del Delete; Move Move/Copy;
1 Size; 2 Format; 3 Lines; 4 Header; 5 Math; 6 Options; 7 Join; 8 Split: 0
```

Figure 23-4. Table grid with the table-editing features

Press F7 Exit to get rid of the table-editing features and return to document-editing mode. You may now enter text and numbers in the cells of the grid.

Figure 23-5 illustrates titles and numbers in the grid. The titles are simply typed in. If your title is too long for a cell, WordPerfect turns the row containing the title into a two-line row. Note that no numbers are used in the titles (for example, "Quarter One" is used, rather than "1st Quarter"). If you use numbers in a column, then perform math for the column, all numbers will be included in the calculation unless you protect the type. How to protect the type is discussed later in this chapter. In the figure, you will also notice that all numbers are left aligned (lined up evenly on the left). Later we will see how to control formatting to allow for a right alignment.

```
File Edit Search Layout Mark Tools Font Graphics Help
```

	Quarter One	Quarter Two	Total	% Saved
Salaries	45,650.00	35,899.00		
Office	3,400.00	3,400.00		
Telephone	1,987.45	1,798.00		
Travel	1,098.42	235.90		
Supplies	2,436.90	1,700.93		
Temporary	9,943.88	19,934.09		
Equipment	19,048.98	12,978.92		
Total				

C:\WP51\DOC\QUAR.WPP   Cell C8 Doc 1 Pg 1 Ln 3.27" Pos 3.7"

Figure 23-5. Headings and numbers in the grid

To enter totals and formulas, you must leave regular document-editing mode by placing your cursor in the table and either pressing Alt-F7 Columns/Tables or selecting Tables, then Edit, from the Layout menu. The editing features reappear on the bottom of the screen. Choose the 5 Math option for totals and formulas. This prompt appears:

Math: 1 Calculate; 2 Formula; 3 Copy Formula; 4 +; 5 =: 6 *:

To enter a vertical (top to bottom) subtotal, place your cursor in the cell for the total and type *4+*. For a total of subtotals, type *5=*. For a grand total of totals, type *6**. The math is automatically calculated.

If you want to enter a formula, select 2 Formula. This prompt appears:

Enter formula:

When you enter a formula, identify each cell in the formula with its designation by column (A, B, etc.) and row (1, 2, etc.). You may use these symbols:

+ addition
− subtraction
* multiplication
/ division

For example, the first formula in our table is illustrated in Figure 23-6. Here, the percentage of savings from first quarter to second quarter is calculated. The cursor is in the cell and the formula appears after

Enter formula:

at the bottom of the screen:

258

B2−C2/B2*100

	Quarter One	Quarter Two	Total	% Saved
Salaries	45,650.00	35,899.00	81,549.00	21.36
Office	3,400.00	3,400.00	6,800.00	0.00
Telephone	1,987.45	1,798.08	3,785.53	9.53
Travel	1,098.42	235.90	1,334.32	78.52
Supplies	2,436.90	1,700.93	4,137.83	30.20
Temporary	9,943.88	19,934.09	29,877.97	−100.47
Equipment	19,048.98	12,978.92	32,027.90	31.87
Total	83,565.63	75,946.92	159,512.55	9.12

File Edit Search Layout Mark Tools Font Graphics Help

=B2−C2/B2*100   Cell E2 Doc 1 Pg 1 Ln 1.59" Pos 6.3"

Figure 23-6. Formula in table

Cell B2 (45,650.00) has cell C2 (35,899.00) subtracted from it. The result is divided by the amount in cell B2 then multi-

plied by 100 to get the percentage. Our result is that the
"Salaries" amount is reduced 21.36 percent from Quarter One
to Quarter Two.

This formula is repeated in each cell in the "% Saved"
column. To repeat a formula, you can type it in, but the
quicker way is to copy it. To do this, make sure your cursor is
on the cell containing the formula you want to copy. After
selecting 5 Math, select 3 Copy Formula. This prompt appears:

`Copy Formula To: 1 Cell; 2 Down; 3 Right:`

In the example, we selected 2 Down and then entered a
number for the number of times to copy the formula. The
appropriate cell designations are entered automatically.

⊘ **Caution:** When you first begin using formulas in
WordPerfect, check the math manually to make sure
the formulas are working correctly. As you become more
confident, you'll need to do less checking. It is always
wise, however, to manually check some work for rea-
sonableness. Some companies have made costly errors
based on a quickly developed math formula that wasn't
checked!

259

Q Creating a Table

1. Press Alt-F7 Columns/
   Tables and then *2* Tables,
   or select Tables from the
   Layout menu. Then press *1*
   Create.

   This prompt appears:
   `Number of Columns:`

2. Enter the number of
   columns for the table and
   press Enter.

   This prompt appears:
   `Number of Rows:`

3. Type in the number of
   rows and press Enter.

   The table grid appears.

4. Press F7 Exit to go into
   document-editing mode.
   Type in your headings and
   numbers.

   The table contents are
   defined.

5. To perform the math, place your cursor in the table. Press Alt-F7 Columns/ Tables and then *2* Tables, or select Tables from the Layout menu.

The options for editing the table appear.

6. Select 5 Math and complete the desired math options.

The math is performed.

Quick Cursor Movement in Tables

Moving around a table by pressing the cursor arrow keys can be time-consuming, so WordPerfect has some quick cursor-movement keys to speed the process. Table 23-2 summarizes the options. Keep this table handy when you begin using tables. As you work with them, you will grow familiar with the keypresses that are most useful to you.

Moving, Copying, or Deleting Table Contents

You can also move, copy, or delete part of a table. If you want to move or copy a block of text into one cell, highlight the cell with Alt-F4 Block. For any move, copy, or delete, either position the cursor to mark the block or place the cursor in the row or column to be affected. Press Ctrl-F4 Move. The options are:

1 Block; 2 Row; 3 Column; 4 Retrieve:

Identify whether you are working with a block, row, or column. (Calling up the Retrieve option allows you to recall text that was already copied; its use is described in Chapter 5.) These options appear:

1 Move; 2 Copy; 3 Delete

Identify whether you are moving, copying, or deleting. If you are moving or copying, place your cursor where you want to insert the text and press Enter, as you would in any WordPer-

Table 23-2. Quick cursor movement in tables

To Go	Press
Single cell movement	
Up one cell	Alt-up arrow
Down one cell	Alt-down arrow
Left one cell	Alt-left arrow, or Shift-Tab, or GoTo followed by left arrow
Right one cell	Tab or Alt-right arrow or GoTo followed by right arrow
Text in a cell	
Start of text in a cell	GoTo followed by up arrow
End of text in a cell	GoTo followed by down arrow
Columns and Rows	
First cell in column	GoTo, then Home, then up arrow or hold down Alt and press Home, then up arrow
Last cell in a column	GoTo, then Home, then down arrow or hold down Alt and press Home, then down arrow
First cell in row	GoTo, then Home, then left arrow or hold down Alt and press Home, then left arrow
Last cell in a row	GoTo, then Home, then right arrow or hold down Alt and press Home, then right arrow
Table	
First cell (upper left)	GoTo, Home, Home, up arrow or hold down Alt and press Home, Home, up arrow
Last cell (lower right)	GoTo, Home, Home, down arrow or hold down Alt and press Home, Home, down arrow

261

fect move or copy. If you move or copy a row or column, it is inserted in the existing table as a row or column. If you move or copy a *block* of text it *replaces* the text *in a single cell*. In other words, the text in the block is fit into one cell and the previous contents of the cell are lost.

⊘ **Caution:** Always save your work before deleting, moving, or copying text. This way, if the result is other than you expected, you can exit the document and retrieve the saved version.

Other Functions Possible with Tables

The earlier discussion described development of a basic table. Considering that WordPerfect tables may be up to 32 columns and 765 rows in size, the table we created was a small one. In this section, we'll look at some functions that enable you to create tables specific to your needs and to streamline your handling of larger tables.

Once a table is created, you access the functions described here by placing your cursor on the table and pressing Alt-F7 Columns/Tables or by selecting Tables, then Edit, from the Layout menu. A menu line of the editing functions appears from which you may make selections. The functions are described briefly in the following discussion. From your experience with WordPerfect you may be able to use these functions through experimentation. But to find more information on a particular function or more detailed information on tables in general, consult an advanced book on WordPerfect.

1 Size: You can use this function to add or delete rows or columns, but there is a better method. Place your cursor in the cell where you want to add or delete a column or row. If you are adding a column, increase the margin to allow for the additional space (otherwise, columns will be reduced in size to fit in the margins). To add, press Insert, then select 1 Row or 2 Column. The row or column will be added before the one on which your cursor rests. To delete a row or column, press Delete then select 1 Row or 2 Column. The row or column on which the cursor rests is deleted.

2 Format: You can change the format of text in a cell, in rows, in columns, or in a block of text highlighted with Alt-F4 Block. You can change the type of text of one or more cells (from numeric to text). Use this feature if the cells include numbers you don't want calculated in with the other numbers. You can also change the attributes of cells (such as bold or normal) or the justification (center, left, or right). For example, in Figure 23-7, the cells with numbers are right justified for a more pleasing appearance. This was accomplished by blocking the cells and then changing the format to right justification. Another cell format is the vertical alignment (top, bottom, or center), though not all printers handle this capability. The vertical alignment change doesn't appear on your screen, but it will appear when printed. Format functions for columns are the width, the attributes, justification, and the number of decimal positions. Row format functions involve the height of the row. Finally, you can lock a cell to prevent future editing.

File Edit Search Layout Mark Tools Font Graphics Help

	Quarter One	Quarter Two	Total	% Saved
Salaries	45,650.00	35,899.00	81,549.00	21.36
Office	3,400.00	3,400.00	6,800.00	0.00
Telephone	1,987.45	1,798.08	3,785.53	9.53
Travel	1,098.42	235.90	1,334.32	78.52
Supplies	2,436.90	1,700.93	4,137.83	30.20
Temporary	9,943.88	19,934.09	29,877.97	-100.47
Equipment	19,048.98	12,978.92	32,027.90	31.87
Total	83,565.63	75,946.92	159,512.55	9.12

=+   Cell B10 Doc 1 Pg 1 Ln 3.83" Pos 2.72"

Figure 23-7. Numeric cells right justified

3 Lines: You can alter the appearance of the lines in the table from completely removing all lines, removing some, or controlling the thickness or appearance (such as using dotted or dashed lines). Just block the lines to control using Alt-F4 Block and then select the Lines function. Choose the option to control the lines within the block. Note that not all printers handle all line types. Experiment with your printer.

4 Header: You can create one or more header rows. For a table that goes past a page break, a header row is printed (but doesn't appear on the regular editing screen) on each page. Just place your cursor on the row above where the header row(s) appear. Then select the header function and *1* On.

5 Math: If you change a formula or numbers, just select 1 Calculation to recalculate the math. As covered earlier in this chapter, you also use this function to enter formulas, copy formulas, and add subtotals, totals, or grand totals.

6 Options: With the options, you can control the space between lines. You can also control the display of negative numbers; for example, changing the display from -1 to (1). Options also allows you to control the placement of the table between margins (you may need to increase the margins first) and to control the shading.

7 Join: You can join several cells to create one cell. Block the cells using Alt-F4 Block, then use the Join function. Text in the cells is separated by tabs.

8 Split: This function allows you to split the cell your cursor is in into your choice of multiple rows or columns.

264

Summary

In this chapter you've learned:

▶ To use WordPerfect's Math function, turn math on; enter text in columns; type in + for subtotals, = for totals, or * for totals of totals; calculate; and turn math off.

▶ WordPerfect's Tables function allows you to create tables with math and formulas.

▶ All math and tables functions are accessed through Alt-F7 Tables/Columns or the Layout menu.

Index

266

D

267

269

I

indenting text, 105-107
    hanging indents, 107
    left and right indent, 107
    left indent, 106
Index command, 229-230
Index Definition screen, 230
indexes, 223-224
    generating, 231-232
    marking and defining, 228-231
initial codes, changing, 112-113
Ins (insert/typeover) key, 24, 40
inserting text, 39-40
[Insert Pg Num:^B] code, 145
Installation screen, 16-18
installing
    printer, 18-19
    WordPerfect, 11-12, 16-20
        networks, 15
[ITALC] [italc] codes, 151
italic characters, 151

J–K

justifying text, 109-111

keyboard, 2, 15-16, 23-24
    moving cursor, 32-35
    selecting from menus, 31
    text blocks, 52
keys
    Alt, 24, 31-32
    arrow, 24
    Backspace, 24, 47-48, 119
    Ctrl, 24
    Delete (Del), 24, 48-49, 119, 121
    End, 24
    Enter, 16, 31-32, 234-235
    Esc, 31-32, 122
    function, 24
    Home, 24
    Ins (insert/typeover), 24, 40
    letter/number/symbol, 24
    Num Lock, 24
    PgDn, 16, 24, 130, 170
    PgUp, 16, 24, 130, 170
    quick movement, 34
    Shift, 24
    Shift-PrtSc, 19
    spacebar, 24
    Tab, 24, 37, 105, 234-235
    tilde (~), 241

270

L

[LARGE] [large] codes, 150
Layout menu, 42, 44, 89-91, 93, 111,
    118, 120, 125, 132-134, 142-145,
    203, 206-207, 209, 252-255, 257,
    259-260, 262
Left Indent (F4) command, 106-107
left tab stop, 117
Left/Right Indent (Shift-F4) command,
    107
Line command, 42, 44, 91, 93, 111,
    118, 120, 132
Line menu, 43
lines, controlling spacing, 111
List Files (F5) command, 78-83, 85,
    101-102, 168, 171-174, 215
List Files menu, 79
List Files screen, 101, 168-175

M

Macro (Alt-F10) command, 217-218
Macro Define (Ctrl-F10) command,
    212, 215, 217-219, 221
macros, 211-221
    defining, 212-216
    describing, 214
    displaying names, 215
    editing, 218-221
    executing, 216-218
    naming, 213
main menu, 27
manual page breaks, 128-129
Margin Release (Shift-Tab) command,
    107, 234-235
margins
    changing, 87-88
    left and right, 91-93
    top and bottom, 90-91
    units of measure, 93-94
Mark menu, 152, 226, 229-231
Mark Text (Alt-F5) command, 152,
    226, 229-231
Mark: Generate screen, 231
marking
    indexes, 228-231
    table of contents, 224-227
master document, 233
math, 251-254
Math command, 252-254
[Math On] code, 252
menus, 5, 27-32

271

273

Reader Feedback Card

Thank you for purchasing this book from SAMS FIRST BOOK series. Our intent with this series is to bring you timely, authoritative information that you can reference quickly and easily. You can help us by taking a minute to complete and return this card. We appreciate your comments and will use the information to better serve your needs.

1. Where did you purchase this book?

☐ Chain bookstore (Walden, B. Dalton)   ☐ Direct mail
☐ Independent bookstore   ☐ Book club
☐ Computer/Software store   ☐ School bookstore
☐ Other _____

2. Why did you choose this book? (Check as many as apply.)

☐ Price   ☐ Appearance of book
☐ Author's reputation   ☐ SAMS' reputation
☐ Quick and easy treatment of subject   ☐ Only book available on subject

3. How do you use this book? (Check as many as apply.)

☐ As a supplement to the product manual   ☐ As a reference
☐ In place of the product manual   ☐ At home
☐ For self-instruction   ☐ At work

4. Please rate this book in the categories below. G = Good; N = Needs improvement; U = Category is unimportant.

☐ Price   ☐ Appearance
☐ Amount of information   ☐ Accuracy
☐ Examples   ☐ Quick Steps
☐ Inside cover reference   ☐ Second color
☐ Table of contents   ☐ Index
☐ Tips and cautions   ☐ Illustrations
☐ Length of book
☐ How can we improve this book?_____
☐ _____

5. How many computer books do you normally buy in a year?

☐ 1–5   ☐ 5–10   ☐ More than 10
☐ I rarely purchase more than one book on a subject.
☐ I may purchase a beginning and an advanced book on the same subject.
☐ I may purchase several books on particular subjects.
☐ (such as _____)

6. Have your purchased other SAMS or Hayden books in the past year? _____
If yes, how many _____

7. Would you purchase another book in the FIRST BOOK series? _____

8. What are your primary areas of interest in business software? _____

☐ Word processing (particularly _____)
☐ Spreadsheet (particularly _____)
☐ Database (particularly _____)
☐ Graphics (particularly _____)
☐ Personal finance/accounting (particularly _____)
☐ Other (please specify _____)

Other comments on this book or the SAMS' book line: _____

_____

Name _____
Company _____
Address _____
City _____ State _____ Zip_____
Daytime telephone number _____
Title of this book _____

Fold here

- -

BUSINESS REPLY MAIL
FIRST CLASS   PERMIT NO. 336   CARMEL, IN

POSTAGE WILL BE PAID BY ADDRESSEE

SAMS

11711 N. College Ave.
Suite 141
Carmel, IN 46032–9839